THE
EDUCATION
OF
TEACHERS

THE
EDUCATION
OF
TEACHERS

Conflict and Consensus

G. K. Hodenfield

&

T. M. Stinnett

PRENTICE-HALL, INC.   A Spectrum Book

Printed in the United States of America

24047-C

The Authors

G. K. HODENFIELD is Education Writer for the Associated Press. His reporting has three times won him the School Bell Award, given by eight national educational organizations for distinguished service in the interpretation of education.

T. M. STINNETT is Executive Secretary, National Commission on Teacher Education and Professional Standards, National Education Association.

Contents

Introduction

This is the story of a historic venture in education. It is the story of three great national conferences aimed at getting the warring segments of American education to sit down together and talk sense about how our teachers should be prepared.

The history of the wrangling is long and bitter. From the founding of the first normal school in the United States in 1839, a continuing debate has persisted among educators as to the best means of educating teachers. But as long as these professional schools confined themselves to turning out teachers for the elementary schools, nobody paid much attention to them. In fact, their admission requirements and curricula were at such low levels as to be beneath the notice of the world of higher education. At the turn of this century, however, the lowly normal schools began to transform themselves into degree-granting teachers colleges. This transformation posed an obvious threat to the liberal arts colleges and universities, who saw in the rise of the teachers colleges the coming invasion of their heretofore exclusive domain in the field of the preparation of high-school teachers. At this point the debate grew into a sullen cold war in higher education. This war had several facets: the liberal arts college vs. the teachers college; the private institution vs. the public institution; above all, the academic professors vs. the education professors. For a half century this feuding smoldered with infrequent pot-shotting.

With the advent of the 1950's and the technological race, the tempo of bickering was stepped up. And by the time the Soviets orbited the first Sputnik, the hassle was already in the early stages of a hot shooting war. With the near panic of the American people over the prospect of falling behind in the arms and technology race, the schools became easy targets for finger pointing. Resentment concerning the accumulated failures and obsolescences in education burst into the angry open and centered upon the lower schools, the seed-bed of our system of mass education.

Everybody in education blamed everybody else. The most convenient scapegoats were the teachers colleges and schools of education, which were attacked by their critics for their alleged easy curricula and poorly prepared teachers. This was only a revival of the sporadic quarreling—which started more than a century ago—about how teachers ought to be educated. The press, the "slicks," and the TV pundits joined in to heap calumny upon the hapless professors of education, who were accused of fostering anti-intellectualism by turning out teachers who were prepared exclusively in methods courses. The campaign to discredit teacher education reached ludicrous new lows in charges and counter-charges. John Dewey became the great whipping boy and the professors of education the stand-ins. By 1958 the situation was rapidly approaching an impasse, with channels of communication sharply closing, and with the charges growing more intemperate. These conditions prompted several of the scholarly societies and professional associations to join in bringing representatives of the warring groups together in annual national conferences of the National Commission on Teacher Education and Professional Standards.

This book is the story of those three conferences—Bowling Green (1958), Kansas (1959), and San Diego (1960). It is told by G. K. Hodenfield, education writer for the Associated Press, who covered the conferences for his wire service. Its purpose is to provide a summarization of this effort as viewed by an impartial, objective observer. Included with the observation of the conferences are also a glimpse at the past, a survey of the present, and a capsule projection of things to come, in this struggle to end the family fight among educators.

The cosponsoring organizations are indebted to the Carnegie Corporation of New York for financial assistance in this co-operative effort. This, and other reports of these conferences, do not, of course, carry any endorsement by the Foundation.

Quotations included herein from the three national and the 1960 regional TEPS conferences are taken from the following publications of the Commission: (1 Volumes 10, 11, and 12 of the *Daily Reporter,* official conference news sheet; (2) the official reports of the Bowling Green, Kansas, and San Diego conferences, entitled *The Education of Teachers: New Perspectives* (1958), *The Education of Teachers: Curriculum Programs* (1959), and *The Education of Teachers: Certification* (1960); and (3) the official report of the 1960 regional conferences, entitled *The Education of Teachers: Considerations in Planning Institutional Programs* (1960).

The undersigned has added only technical materials for students and technicians in education.

T. M. Stinnett

PART I

By G. K. Hodenfield

CHAPTER ONE

The War of the Academic Worlds

It was like asking the Hatfields and the McCoys to get together for a Sunday dinner—or like asking the Republicans and the Democrats to hold a joint convention.

That was the Bowling Green Conference of 1958. Ever since the turn of the century, liberal arts professors and scholars had been feuding with their colleagues in teacher education, and suddenly they all were being asked to sit down together to discuss the improvement of teacher training.

It was not just a matter of whether the conference would really get anything accomplished. There was the very real question whether the conference could even be held together for its scheduled four days. When the 1,025 participants packed their bags for Bowling Green they left plenty of room for their prejudices and their biases; the set-up was made to order for an academic version of a Pier 6 brawl.

Why was it so important that the Bowling Green Conference be held? Why was it so imperative that it succeed? To answer these questions we must take a brief look at the history of teacher education in this country, the arguments that raged, and the bitterness that spread over more than half a century.

The idea that teachers need special preparation for their jobs was slow to catch on in this country, although suggestions to that effect were heard as far back as the middle of the eighteenth century. A historian has pointed out:

It was nearly two centuries after Massachusetts had ordered the establishment of schools before the state (in 1839) provided for the training of teachers for those schools. After Connecticut had provided for schools it was nearly 175 years before there was even a suggestion that the state establish an institution exclusively for training teachers, and it was several decades later before such a school was provided.[1]

[1] Edgar W. Knight, *Education in the United States*, 3rd ed. (Boston: Ginn and Company, 1951), p. 310.

By 1870, the idea of special teacher education was generally accepted, especially for elementary-school teachers, and normal schools were springing up everywhere. But this was a far cry from the teachers colleges which followed. Students generally went directly into normal school from elementary school and Knight says that "As late as 1900 the typical normal school provided only two years of work beyond the high school." [2]

When courses in pedagogy or education finally found their way to the doors of the colleges and universities, they were generally reluctantly admitted, assigned subordinate places, and kept in humility as long as possible. Some of the conditions which made them unwelcome in the colleges and universities also helped to keep them subordinate. The pioneer professors of pedagogy in these institutions were doubtless often effective and were generally picturesque, but they were not always standardized and orthodox products of the colleges and universities. Many of them had not bowed the knee to the gods of the graduate school. They were innocent of the idolatry of doctoral dissertations and the methods of scientific research. Their methods were anecdotic and reminiscent of their experience in teaching and managing schools. Organized materials for pedagogical instruction were scarce until after 1900, and the practical experience of the early professors of pedagogy formed a large part of the materials of their courses. The standards of their work, which was limited to a few fields, were not always high—probably little if any higher than the normal school standards—and their claim to scientific character could not always be supported.

These and other conditions caused courses in pedagogy or education early to fall under the heavy prejudice of other departments. They still suffer from this affliction.[3]

Things did not get better after the turn of the century—they got worse. When the Russians sent Sputnik I whizzing about over our startled heads in the fall of 1957, the division between the liberal arts scholars and the teacher educators erupted into an all-out campaign of invective and vituperation. Extremists on one side grabbed the floor (and the headlines) to proclaim that teachers were being taught *how* to teach but not *what* to teach and that, really, if you knew your subject well enough, you could teach it. Extremists on the other side retorted that if you really knew how to teach, you could teach anything. Saner folk on both sides pointed out that a good teacher ought to know *what* to teach as well as *how* to teach, but their voices were lost in the din.

One highly respected scholar wrote an article denouncing teacher education as "scattershot scholarship" which produces teachers like the

[2] *Ibid.*, p. 329.
[3] *Ibid.*, p. 335.

one who reportedly told his class: "You oughtta study your Latin instead of griping about it. You never know but what you'll wanna travel in Latin America some day." (There may be, somewhere in these United States, just such a teacher. If there is, no one would rather get him out of the business than his fellow teachers.)

So fast and furiously did the charges and counter-charges fly, so bitter became the arguments, that a nationally circulated magazine asked two men to answer the question, "How Well Are Our Teachers Being Taught?" John Keats, author of *Schools Without Scholars* and the father of three children, replied, "Never Worse," and allowed as follows:[4]

If your Johnny can't read, write, or do arithmetic, it may be due to the fact that his teacher can't do these things well herself. And the reason *she* can't do them is that *her* instructors in teachers college were told she should be taught other things instead.

In teachers college, they told her that all children should not be expected to read, write, or do arithmetic, anyway. She heard it was more important for Johnny to be well adjusted and happy than it was for him to be asked to use his head. In teachers college she spent far more time learning to ventilate a classroom than she spent learning anything she might be asked to teach. Then she was told she could teach students a foreign language without being able to read, write, or pronounce it herself. Finally, she was warned that if she made a brilliant record in what formal studies there were in her teachers college, she might not be allowed to teach at all.

Keats described a mythical institution called "Fairly Normal," which he said was a "sample" teachers college in New York State's university system. He quoted the dean of education there as saying: "Good teachers are produced solely by scientific teaching methods. We say 'We teach children, not subjects,' and we say 'A good teacher can teach anything.' "

Thus, Keats continues:

A future English teacher may spend one-third of his time learning How to Teach, and as little as one-seventh of his time studying English. For this reason, the English courses are hasty surveys with no emphasis on mastery of any particular phase of the material. I plucked a paper at random from a pile of Fairly Normal freshman essays. It was eight paragraphs long, entitled "How to Shot a Bow." Unfortunately, the author will not have an opportunity to increase his proficiency, because Fairly Normal requires only one semester in English composition. Four years from now he may be teaching

---

[4] John Keats, "How Well Are Our Teachers Being Taught? Never Worse!" *Better Homes and Gardens* 36: 51-52; May 1958. (Copyright © by Meredith Publishing Company, Des Moines, Iowa. All rights reserved.)

composition to your child. Or perhaps he may be teaching French, which he did not study in either high school *or* at Fairly Normal, because teachers colleges believe good teachers can teach literally anything.

.   .   .

There is no apparent limit to the lengths to which this mindlessness may be carried. A lesson on "proper classroom ventilation," for instance, is not just a five-minute lecture, but a separate course, the gist of which is that classroom air should be kept fresh and at a constant temperature. I regret having to say I am serious.

Now, these are pretty strong statements. It's enough to make you wonder how the kids even manage to read the sports pages these days.

The same issue of the magazine carried a contrary view by Robert H. Beck, professor of history and philosophy of education at the University of Minnesota. Professor Beck claimed that teachers had never been trained better.[5]

Contrary to a highly vocal segment of public opinion, teachers colleges are not a waste of time for the men and women enrolled in them, nor do they stand in the way of your Johnny's learning to read, write, and do arithmetic. There is, in fact, good reason to believe that today's professionally trained teachers are the best teachers our schools have ever had, and not only can Johnny learn from them, but he can learn faster and better.

Proof of this is found in a study by Professor Benjamin S. Bloom of the University of Chicago. He compared sample scores of millions of high-school seniors taking the General Education Development tests in 1943 with those taking them in 1955. The GED has five sections—English composition, social studies, natural science, literature, and mathematics. Professor Bloom found that in all five areas the students' knowledge of the subject was greater than it had been 12 years earlier.

.   .   .

Anyone who is surprised by these findings has probably fallen victim to rumors that today's teachers can't teach—that the education courses they take in teachers colleges are totally useless, and that these courses monopolize their time and prevent them from learning anything worth teaching. It isn't so.

First of all, prospective teachers don't spend all their hours learning How to Teach. The National Education Association's *Manual on Certification Requirements*[6] shows that high-school instructors in most states need no more

[5] Robert H. Beck, "How Well Are Our Teachers Being Taught? Never Better!" *Better Homes and Gardens* 36: 51+; May 1958. (Copyright © by Meredith Publishing Company, Des Moines, Iowa. All rights reserved.)

[6] W. Earl Armstrong and T. M. Stinnett, *A Manual on Certification Requirements for School Personnel in the United States,* 1959 ed. (Washington: National Education Association, National Commission on Teacher Education and Professional Standards, 1959).

than 16 or 18 semester hours of education courses. This is roughly one-seventh of a normal four-year college education. In contrast, the average requirement for state certification as a high school teacher is 24 semester hours in English, modern foreign languages, or social studies for anyone who is to teach those subjects. And these minimum requirements are usually exceeded by most students. Future elementary school teachers ordinarily take about a fourth of their college study in education courses—considerably more than do budding high school instructors. But this increased emphasis isn't strange, considering the difficulty of imparting basic concepts to very young children.

. . .

As an example of a methods course that has come under some ridicule, let's take the teaching of reading. Should an elementary school teacher take such a course? Surely she can read; why can't she teach reading? If you try this with your own six-year-old, you'll soon see the difficulty. The sound of the letter "A" will be the first thing to throw you. Which of the eight sounds listed in the pronunciation key of a dictionary should be taught first? "A" is for "apple," true. But "A" is also for "ace" and for "axe," not to mention "alphabet," which has two "A's," each sounded differently. Even at this first stage of instruction, you may give up, wondering how teachers ever do it.

Well, they do it because they've had a course teaching them when to introduce phonics and how to teach them—and when and how to teach blends, digraphs, variant endings, root words, compounds, prefixes, suffixes, and syllabification. All these things, they have learned, enter into effective word recognition.

Professor Beck makes a strong case for the teachers colleges. But, human nature being what it is—and because the Russians got their earth satellite into orbit before we did—it's likely that what Mr. Keats said is what most readers remembered.

The magazine, in a commendable effort to ferret out the truth, gave each author a chance, in the same issue, to answer the other. Since Mr. Keats' charges were the most eye-catching, let's see what Professor Beck had to say about them.

Mr. Keats says there are teachers who spend far more time learning to ventilate a classroom than learning anything they might be asked to teach.

This statement is false. I cannot conceive of any college—not even the most dismal two-year normal school—where this claim would hold true.

. . .

Mr. Keats says Johnny may be learning French from a teacher who did not study French herself in either high school or college.

I doubt whether there is an institution in the United States that will recommend for certification, as a teacher of French, a student who has not had at least six or seven courses in college French. The large majority of colleges preparing teachers require a major in French (or whatever the subject for which the student is to be certified). The college major almost always exceeds the minimum requirements for state certification.

.   .   .

Mr. Keats says Johnny's teacher heard it was more important for Johnny to be well adjusted than it was for him to be asked to use his head.

A teacher who helps the personal adjustment of a student is not thereby preventing him from using his head. Mr. Keats accepts the mistaken notion that knowledge must be boring (or teaching methods harsh) in order to be intellectually nourishing. Quite the contrary. There is good reason to believe that a pupil is free to use his head when he is not distracted by persistent anxiety or angry rebelliousness. Rather than resisting his teacher and his studies, a happy, adjusted student has energy to use in learning.

Mr. Keats says that Johnny's teacher has been told not to expect all children to read, write, or do arithmetic.

And it is a fact that some children *can't* learn to read, write, or do arithmetic. Johnny's teacher was told that *most* children, however, can learn the three R's, and she has been taught how to assist that learning. High marks made by her students in dozens of achievement tests prove that she has learned well, too.

The debate between Mr. Keats and Professor Beck has been cited at some length to illustrate the areas of disagreement about teacher education. Some of the charges against teachers colleges are valid; some are so wild as to be fantastic. Some of the charges have hit home; some have been aimed at the wrong target. In every such dispute, spokesmen for both sides have tended to grab at an isolated example and to try to make a federal case of it.

There may well be, as Mr. Keats said, a teachers college in the state of New York such as the one called "Fairly Normal." Whatever its real name might be, it is not "State University of New York College of Education" at Albany, for instance. The college catalogue shows that a student preparing there for a high-school teaching career is required to take 22 semester hours of professional education courses, *including* 6 hours of student teaching. He also must take 36 semester hours of general education. In addition to this 58 hours, if he is going to teach English he must have 31 semester hours in that subject. If he is going to teach a modern foreign language he must have 29 semester hours in that. If he is going to teach history and social science, he must have 36 semester hours of that. And this is typical of all teachers colleges in New York.

It is true, too, that your Johnny may some day be taught French by a teacher who is not qualified. There is an ever-growing demand for language teachers, now that the foreign language program is being extended downward into the elementary grades. In Kansas, at the time of the Bowling Green Conference, a high-school French class could be taught by an English teacher, for instance, who had had a minimum of six semester hours of French in college. That is a one-year college course—about the time it might take some students to learn to say in French, "The pen of my aunt is on the table."

It is a sad fact, as the Modern Language Association reported to the U. S. Office of Education in mid-1960, that *not one* of the fifty states requires foreign language teachers to speak the language they teach. Eleven states have no requirements for teaching a language in an elementary school. In the words of one educator, "This is substandard, even by substandard standards." State requirements have been getting stiffer in recent years. Even so, state certification of language teachers leaves much to be desired.

So whom do you blame if the teacher of French lacks the proper preparation? The teacher herself, who majored in English, and planned and hoped to teach nothing else? The principal or superintendent of the school, who cannot find a fully qualified French teacher, and has to do the best he can because of the pressure by parents for a high-school course in French? The school board, which will not put up the money to hire a full-time French teacher? Or the public, which will not let the school board spend the necessary money?

Or do you, in Kansas, blame the School of Education of the University of Kansas? The university insists that to be certified as a high-school French teacher a student must have 34 to 35 semester hours of French (plus 22 semester hours of professional education).

This is *not* to whitewash the schools of education and the teachers colleges. Far from it. Some of them go overboard in requiring professional education courses for their students. Consider, for instance, these requirements for prospective elementary teachers at one teachers college in the East.

Courses	*Semester Hours*
Professional Orientation	3
Audio-Visual Education	2
General Psychology	3
Educational Psychology and Evaluative Techniques	3
Student Teaching and Direction of Student Activities	12
Professional Practicum Including School Law	2
Music for Elementary Grades	2
Teaching Music in Elementary Grades	3
Science for the Elementary Grades	3
Teaching of Elementary Science	3
Art for Elementary Grades	2
Teaching Art in the Elementary Grades	3

Courses	Semester Hours
Teaching of Language	3
Teaching of Social Studies and Geography	3
Teaching of Health	2
Children's Literature	3
Teaching of Arithmetic	3
Child Development	3
Teaching of Reading	3
Total	61

This particular college also requires a minimum of 42 to 53 semester hours in general education, which can be taken from the following fields: English, health and physical education, history of civilization, basic physical science, world geography, American government, speech, literature, basic biology, introduction to art, history of the United States and the state (in which the college is located).

Practically all educators will agree that 61 semester hours of professional education is a bit much, even for a prospective elementary-school teacher. But there are further dangers to such a program. The college "requires" 61 semester hours of education, but does not set any maximum. Thus, a student can take as many as 80 hours of professional courses. If the same student fulfills his or her general education requirements by concentrating heavily on health and physical education, introduction to art, and speech (all of them excellent courses in themselves), your little Johnny for sure is going to have a teacher who knows the *how* but not the *what* of teaching.

This is a ridiculous aspect of higher education, and it is not limited just to teacher education programs. In my own field, for instance, I have met newspapermen who took every journalism course they could schedule to the neglect of the general education that any newspaperman needs. Later they have found themselves writing politics with no background in political science, serving as foreign correspondents when they know nothing of world history, or writing a business news story without benefit of a single college course in economics. Like some teachers, they got fine training at college, but a poor education. The same probably is true in other fields. In this connection, Richard M. Nixon suggests that anyone planning a career in politics should concentrate heavily on the humanities, with only a smattering of political science courses.

The critics of the teachers colleges contend, with some justification, that too many of them overdo the "techniques" of teaching, that there is too much stress on methods with only a passing glance at the subject matter. There is often a tendency in a teachers college or school of education to set up a separate course for every knack and art a teacher should have, instead of realistically lumping a number of them into one course. In the example, cited earlier, of the college requiring 61 hours of professional education, could not "Art for Elementary Grades" (2 semester hours) and "Teaching of Art in the Elementary Grades" (3 semester hours) be taught as one course? Could not many of the individual courses in methods be gathered together in some sort of a block course that would take less time?

The teachers themselves, caught in the middle of this hassle, often complain that their education courses are boring, monotonous, and repetitious. That is, indeed, unfortunate, because they need not be.

For every professional educator who defends the proliferation of methods courses, you will find a scholar who says they should all be washed out of the curriculum.

Paul Woodring, consultant to the Ford Foundation's Fund for the Advancement of Education, dealt with the professional skills needed to organize and manage a classroom in a speech to the American Society of Newspaper Editors, meeting in Washington in April, 1958.

To see the need for these skills, ask yourself what you would do if you were placed in front of a class of third-graders tomorrow. What would you teach? What books would you use? How would you organize the day? What methods would you use in teaching reading and arithmetic? Perhaps you know the answers to all these questions, but many beginning teachers do not—and this includes many teachers with an excellent liberal arts background.

Only a few months before the Bowling Green Conference convened, *Life* Magazine[7] editorially explored the problems of education and blamed almost everything on John Dewey and his disciples.

The Deweyites . . . transformed conditioning techniques into ends in themselves. As they tracked through U. S. education, teachers colleges assumed the dignity of lamaseries. They called their system science, but they worshipped its doctrines like a cult. In thousands of schools, teachers were denied the chance of learning more about their subjects in favor of compulsory education courses in how to teach them.

.   .   .

By their own trusted empirical test, the poor performance of their students has proved the educationists wrong. U. S. high-school students are plain ignorant of the things grammar-school students would have known a generation ago. Years of barren discussion courses in English have made a whole generation chronically incoherent in the English language (the mutterings of a U. S. teen-ager trying to discuss his beliefs generally sound like a

---

[7] "The Deeper Problem in Education" (Editorial), *Life.* Copyright © 1958 by Time, Inc.

sanitized version of Elvis Presley). By substituting "projects" for study, the
educationists have soothed students' curiosity, but left them with little intellectual patience for solving problems. Cut off from any but the most obvious
contact with his tradition, e.g., an occasional project visit to the local court-
house, the student has lost his sense of history, at a time when his country
needs this most. Surely the history of the Crusades can give a young American a better grasp of the problems implicit in the U.N. or NATO than
dressing up as a Pakistani delegate in an imitation U.N. assembly at school.

.   .   .

We cannot expect to cure such lopsided standards just by giving teachers
the pay they deserve, building the schools we need, and ordering up more
science courses. A few important steps *can* be taken by state and local
authorities. For one thing, most of our state teachers colleges should be
abolished as such and converted into liberal arts colleges, with subordinate
education departments. There must also be some drastic upgrading of curriculum requirements.

But most of all we need to do some thinking about the true ends of education. The worthwhile innovations in method brought by Dewey's educationists should be kept. But their exclusive devotion to techniques and group
adjustment should never again be allowed to hide the fact that American
education exists first of all to educate the individual in a body of learning,
with a tradition and purpose behind it. A man so educated is far better
equipped as a democratic citizen than the merely "well adjusted." For he will
have not only the social ease to make his civilization comfortable, but the
intellectual discipline to help save it.

Frederick C. Neff, professor of education at Rutgers University, was
one of many educators who took umbrage at *Life*'s remarks. Professor
Neff's reply was printed in *Phi Delta Kappan*,[8] journal of the professional fraternity for men in education. For a number of reasons which
need not be explored here, the national circulation of *Phi Delta
Kappan* falls considerably below that of *Life,* so it is most unlikely
that all those who read the *Life* article also read Professor Neff's
reaction.

Dewey is derided for advocating aimlessness in education. What he actually
said was that "acting with an aim is all one with acting intelligently."
Whereas it is claimed that Dewey de-emphasized subject matter, he in
fact said that "what is needed in the new education is *more* attention, not
less, to subject matter and to progress in technique. But when I say more, I
do not mean more in quantity of the same old kind."

.   .   .

In respect to the Luce proposal that most state teachers colleges be
abolished, it requires no philosophical depth to detect the innuendo that

[8] Frederick C. Neff, "John Dewey and the Luce Ends of Education," *Phi Delta
Kappan* 40: 130-31; December 1958.

schools and colleges of education in general and, indeed, such courses as are designed to prepare young people for the profession of teaching should likewise be abolished.

· · ·

While we are about it, why not urge the abolition of our law and medical schools? Why not hold that the prospective lawyer needs no particular training in arguing a case, no special knowledge of legal processes? Why not turn him loose with nothing more than a set of books and some memorized cases and let him sink or swim? He may have to repeat all the mistakes that his predecessors have made, and it may take him a lifetime to do it; his clients may suffer accordingly, and he may never succeed in earning a living—but at least he will have been spared the nuisance of mastering the techniques and procedures of his profession.

Why not present the prospective physician or surgeon with a series of liberal arts courses in the history of medical lore and forego training him in the techniques of how to make an adequate diagnosis, how to administer an anaesthetic, or how to perform a successful operation? No sane person would seriously consider permitting a medical man to practice without a license or to engage in his profession without a mastery of whatever techniques are necessary for the successful performance of his professional duties. Yet, if teacher-training institutions and, by implication, teaching certification are to be abolished, then any housewife, truck driver, or degree-holder who has accumulated an arbitrary number of "subject-matter credits" would be permitted to practice in our schools, regardless of whatever harm might come to the youngsters from his teaching ineptness. It seems just a bit odd that such a proposal in law or medicine would be laughed out of court, while an analogous proposal in education can receive so serious a hearing.

And thus we have two sides of the story—or have we? Aside from its attack on some Dewey-eyed professional educators, *Life* made one concrete proposal: "Most of our state teachers colleges should be abolished as such and converted into liberal arts colleges, with subordinate education departments." And it added: "The worthwhile innovations in methods brought by Dewey's educationists should be kept."

Was *Life* really asking that *all* schools and colleges of education be abolished, and that students preparing to be teachers be given *no* courses whatever in the methods of teaching? It would not appear so, yet Neff professed to see that bogeyman in the closet.

This illustrates a sensitivity on the part of the professional educators that has made it difficult over the years for them to sit down with the liberal arts scholars and professors and work out their differences. It is not just a case of "You're either with us or against us." It is a case of "You're either 100 per cent for us or you must be dead set against us." Perhaps this sensitivity is justified when you remember for how long the scholars have been looking down their noses at "those teacher training people." Justified or not, it has served only to make a bad situation worse.

In this connection, let us consider Vice-Admiral Hyman G. Rickover, the acid-tongued critic of the state of public education in this country today. To the vast majority of educators, Admiral Rickover is "that man who builds submarines," just as choleric businessmen by the thousands used to refer to President Franklin D. Roosevelt as "that man in the White House." One of Admiral Rickover's pet targets has been the National Education Association, and the feeling is unanimously mutual.

And yet, Admiral Rickover believes in federal aid to education. So does the NEA. Admiral Rickover believes in the use of federal funds to pay teachers' salaries; so does the NEA. Admiral Rickover wants special programs for the nation's gifted children; so does the NEA. Admiral Rickover wants tougher high-school courses in science, math, and foreign languages; so does the NEA. Admiral Rickover wants teaching recognized as the noblest profession of them all; so does the NEA. There are many areas in which the admiral and the NEA disagree, and disagree violently, but also there are some areas in which they think alike. The point is, neither will publicly admit seeing eye to eye with the other on anything.

How does Admiral Rickover stand on teacher education? Here is an excerpt from the Admiral's oft-quoted testimony on Capitol Hill in August, 1959.

I would suggest that we aim at having teachers in the last three years of high school who have had the equivalent of a first-rate legal education; that would be a bachelor's degree plus three years postgraduate study in their chosen subjects. Elementary teachers would need somewhat less knowledge of subject matter and more of pedagogy. All teachers need some special instruction in pedagogy and a good deal of practice teaching. We might consider copying the internship in education which is common abroad—teacher candidates practicing under the supervision of experienced teachers before they take on a class all by themselves.

Certainly Admiral Rickover acknowledges the value of methods courses for both elementary- and secondary-school teachers—although not necessarily of the type and number now available in schools and colleges of education. His suggestion for three years of postgraduate work for high-school teachers, and for teaching internships, is not far from what many professional educators themselves are calling for, as we shall see later.

Part of the trouble may be that both sides tend to exaggerate. There is nothing that will irritate a professional educator more than the charge that courses in fly-casting and baton-twirling are replacing the Three R's. There are such courses in some schools, but you have to look long and hard to find them. On the other hand, the critics of American education are equally annoyed when they hear someone say that the public schools in this country are about as near-perfect as the human mind and hand can devise. The layman can only assume that both sides are wrong and have been led astray by their zeal to make a point.

The internecine fight between the professional educators and the liberal arts scholars took on new vigor and new venom with the advent of the earth satellites in the fall of 1957. At first glance, this seems like a ridiculous reason for educators to step up the tempo of their intra-mural quarrels. But Sputnik I had hit the American public squarely in the face with a most uncomfortable fact: those Russians were not the stolid, unimaginative peasants we thought them to be. They had beaten us into space and so—the argument went—it must be the fault of our schools. When the heat of public indignation was turned on the schools, members of the educational family started defending them-selves with wild swings which as often as not landed on a professional cousin.

Along about then, someone must have remembered the words of the dean of the Graduate School of the University of Minnesota, who in 1953 had said:

> The time has come in American education for the scholars of subject-matter specialization and those who profess professional education to find common ground and to grapple unitedly with the problems of education that are crucial to the oncoming generations of our people. Misunderstand-ings, where they befog the scene, should be swept away. Weakness, where it is discerned, should lead, not to epithets, but to efforts to build strength. Bases for mutual confidence and co-operation should be looked for. If there is alignment into enemy camps, why not mutually explore assumed reasons for hostility and make sure that we have, in truth, picked the right enemies to fight.[9]

Sometime in the next few years was born the idea of a national con-ference, calling the warring worlds of education to an armistice meet-ing. Dr. T. M. Stinnett, executive secretary of the National Commis-sion on Teacher Education and Professional Standards (NCTEPS), a commission of the National Education Association, was in on the

---

[9] Theodore C. Blegen, "Toward a Common Front" (Address Before the Duke University Centennial Conference on Teacher Training) *Historical Papers of the Trinity College Historical Society* (Durham, N. C.: Duke University Press, 1953), p. 21.

project from the start. Here is the story of the birth of the Bowling Green Conference, in his words.[10]

The origin and development of this co-operative effort may have considerable historic significance, yet many of the initial details are obscure. With respect to the beginnings and evaluation, as with so many significant developments in the field of education, no one ever seems to take the time to record precisely the moment of emergence of the idea, or its nurture. Even this writer, as close as he has been to the development, is hazy as to how the movement really got underway. He is unable to identify the individual who first shaped the idea. It is easy to recall that the idea emerged at the crest of the internecine controversy, at which point it was obvious to everyone that the interchange of invectives was producing no fruitful results. Educators were engaged in a hot, civil war, and the sensational press and the "slicks" were squeezing every drop of indignation, calumny, and vituperation from the situation. Some interests with axes to grind pitched into the controversy, further obscuring the facts. Somewhere along this tortuous road—just when and where we do not know precisely—there began to emerge a soberness among the various scholarly societies and the associations representing the teaching profession in the elementary schools, and among their executive officers; and a wiser approach began to take shape. In a sentence, the essence of that approach was that, although everyone concluded that reforms and improvements in the light of new conditions and demands upon education were essential, the current controversy obviously was going to be unproductive of results other than providing a field day for those interested in getting the ultimate in mileage out of charges and counter-charges. From this contretemps there began to emerge the notion that significant reforms were not going to be obtained over the prone bodies of the members of the teaching profession itself; that no amount of "Madison Avenue arousements" were going to stampede the profession and the public, and that no amount of vituperation was going to achieve dedicated commitment to revision. On the other hand, the members of the profession who teach in the elementary and secondary schools began to sense that we had indeed come upon new times, with new implications for education, and that stubborn resistance to change was not the answer. They began to sense that there were great resources among the scholars in the various disciplines which would greatly strengthen the drive for revision and refinement. And most significant of all, they came to believe that, for the first time, these scholarly groups were really interested in helping. Thus, some notion of the potential power of a partnership of voluntary and concerted efforts as essential to the upgrading of the school system—a system which does not move by edict or by authoritarian pronouncements—began to be substantial.

As far as we can recall, the first forward step in bringing about a fusion of effort arose from a survey of one of the learned societies of the graduate offerings in its field for teachers. The survey convinced officials of this organization that the house-cleaning was not needed in the field of professional

---

[10] T. M. Stinnett, "The Hopeful Trilogy" (Editorial), *Journal of Teacher Education* 11: 131-32; June 1960.

education alone, as the clamor indicated, and that a general across-the-board reassessment was imperative. This revelation was the impetus for a number of informal meetings of the executive secretaries of several of the professional associations and of the learned societies whose headquarters are in Washington. In one of these informal conversations, the idea was developed that the National TEPS Commission already had the machinery for touching, in one way or another, directly or indirectly, more than a million practitioners in the elementary and secondary schools. This is the basic reason that the Commission was chosen as the instrument for these concerted efforts. By joining forces, the learned societies could bring to bear the participation of most of the sectors of American education with whom the Commission had little contact. No planning was done beyond the phrasing of the idea. The executive officers of these cosponsoring learned societies took the initiative, and were instrumental in securing modest financial support of the venture from the Carnegie Corporation of New York. A Steering Committee was established, with a representative of each of the eight cosponsoring organizations. (Later an additional group joined the effort.) The National TEPS Commission wholeheartedly endorsed the venture. The Steering Committee and the Commission have managed to see eye-to-eye in every step of the process. There were, from time to time, differences of opinion about organizational procedures, of course, but in each instance these were worked upon until there was complete reconcilement.

The Bowling Green Conference of 1958 was not the first effort toward getting scholars to participate in the affairs of teacher education. Many national meetings, on a limited basis but with the same general purposes, had been held. But Bowling Green in 1958 *was* the first large-scale national effort to involve representatives of all areas of education from the kindergarten through the graduate school.

It might be in order here to clarify some terminology. It seems to be the custom, in discussions of teacher education and arguments about methods versus subject matter, to refer to those whose primary business is the education and training of teachers as "professional educators." Those who teach in other fields—professors of history, literature, chemistry—are known as "scholars." This is loose usage of the English language. By the very manner in which they earn a living the college professors are "professional educators," and one should not have to argue that there are many scholarly men in the field of teacher education. (We might also make a case for the proposition that there is, or should be, considerable general education or "subject matter" in any good methods course, and that a future teacher should be able to learn something about methods from any professor in general education.)

And so they came to Bowling Green: teachers, professors, administrators, representatives of state departments of education, laymen, and spokesmen for state and national education associations.

They arrived only a few days after publication of a report by the Rockefeller Brothers Fund, Inc., which bluntly warned the nation that:

Perhaps the greatest problem facing American education is the widely held view that all we require are a few more teachers, a few more buildings, a little more money. Such an approach will be disastrous. . . . An educational system grudgingly and tardily patched to meet the needs of the moment will be perpetually out of date. We must build for the future in education as daringly and aggressively as we built other aspects of our national life in the past.[11]

Looking back now, it is clear that the Bowling Green Conference had to be a success. Because it was, the Kansas Conference of 1959 and the San Diego Conference of 1960 were also successful. Because all three were successful, there may be a bright new future for American education. But there was not much real confidence in the future when the first participants checked in at the Bowling Green State University Student Union on June 24, 1958.

[11] *The Pursuit of Excellence: Education and The Future of America* (New York: Doubleday & Company, Inc., 1958), p. 33. Copyright © 1958 by Rockefeller Brothers Fund, Inc. Reprinted by permission of Doubleday & Company, Inc.

CHAPTER TWO

"Always There Stands the Teacher . . ."

They came to Bowling Green. There were those with high optimism, who were certain all the problems of education could be quickly solved; there were the mockers who came expecting nothing, but figuring they had nothing to lose—they soon found they both were wrong. What was it all about, and what happened? The Bowling Green Conference of 1958 was about "What to Teach" and "How to Teach," about methods and subject matter, about certification and accreditation, about professional education and general education and special education. But most of all it was about "How do we produce a better teacher?"

The teacher was the focus of the conference, and the anchor. Extremists from both sides of the divided education world could fly off in all directions—and sometimes did—but always they were brought back to earth by the one overriding interest of all participants: turning out better teachers.

Historians of the future may well call Bowling Green a turning point in American education. It was that. But it was more, too. It was an assembly point where divergent armies joined forces and began marching forward together. It was a burial ground for old grudges and feuds (even if all of them were not properly interred). It was a beginning.

There were no spectacular achievements at Bowling Green—at least not of the sort that bring out the big, black headlines and cause breathless radio and television announcers to say, "We interrupt this program to bring you a special news bulletin." It has been said that it would be easier to move Lake Michigan to Nebraska than to change the course of American education. This is debatable, perhaps, but it certainly is true that no educational conference itself is ever going to change American education. The change comes after, not during, the conference.

In the official report of the Bowling Green Conference it was noted:

For those who have recently been startled by warnings as to the inadequacy of the American system of education, the results of any educational conference, no matter how solid, are likely to seem insufficient. If a half-dozen of the major reforms strongly advocated at Bowling Green were immediately put into effect in a hundred teacher training programs, they would scarcely produce their intended results in less than a decade—at a rate, that is, too slow to satisfy those who believe that immediate and fundamental changes are necessary if we are to avert national disaster.

But there *was* progress at Bowling Green, just because people sat down together and talked things over—and this in itself may have been a spectacular achievement. Certainly the harmony and the co-operation displayed there surprised many. A conference official later wrote:[1]

As one looks back on that conference, several factors stand out. The first is the dramatic air of tension which existed as the 1,000 participants arrived for the conference. The air was electric—something like the tension that prevails in a college football stadium on the day of the big game, when all the dope indicates that the issue will be settled by the happenstance of the direction a bounding ball might take. This tension, of course, was heightened by gratuitous publicity screaming for conflict. It was obvious to the thoughtful onlooker that one incendiary statement or one violently partisan headline could have blown the frail and untried craft of the conference completely out of the water before it got underway. Fortunately, however, the participants met each other openly and squarely, refusing to lose their tempers and insisting upon intellectual discussion of their differences and the problems of common concern. As the conference completed its first day one could almost hear a vast sigh of relief. The ground had been laid for fruitful discussion; a rapport had been established by which the most controversial, difficult problems could be laid upon the top of the table and discussed openly and freely.

It is difficult to imagine that any other national conference will ever be held in which such an air of sustained tension will be so evident. As the conference progressed, the participants' innate fairness and devotion to the facts took over; there was an obvious shedding of stereotypes, implanted by statements of extremists and sustained propaganda campaigns. There was, on both sides, an honest acknowledgment of many errors and a great feeling of excitement in discovering a mutual concern and desire to get on with the business of improving our schools. Of course, these feelings were not universal, but general.

The teacher was the focus, and the anchor. Jack Allen, professor of history at George Peabody College for Teachers, spoke for every man and woman at Bowling Green when he declared:

[1] T. M. Stinnett, "The Hopeful Trilogy," *Journal of Teacher Education* 11: 132-33; June 1960.

One of the prime functions of the school, indeed the chief function, is to provide a setting within which boys and girls can grow intellectually. This can only be accomplished through the learner's association with information, knowledge, facts. Books can help. So can laboratories. So can numerous other types of learning materials. *But always there stands the teacher, always on the stage, often front and center. What he knows can make a difference. What he does not know can be an irreparable loss.*

I suppose all of us old enough to be subject to nostalgia can remember a teacher who made the difference. I was lucky; I had two such teachers.

Mrs. Alma Wedberg was my fourth, fifth, and sixth grade teacher in a little two-room country school outside Redlands, California. I remember few of the facts she taught me (although to my dying day I'll remember the location of the Tigris and Euphrates Rivers). The thing I remember most about Mrs. Wedberg was her ability to make the whole wide world and everything in it and about it interesting and exciting. Later, in high school at Glenwood, Iowa, I had Miss Dorothy Sherman as an English teacher in both my junior and senior years. Again, few of the facts she tried so hard to pound into my head remain, but Miss Sherman introduced me to the joys of writing, the *fun* of trying to make a sentence and a paragraph say just exactly what I wanted it to say. This was in the midst of the Depression, and I had no more idea of going on to college than I had of writing a book about teacher education. This did not matter to Miss Sherman; she worked as hard with me as if I were a crown prince and she a tutor to the Royal Family.

It was inevitable, with two such teachers, that I became a newspaperman. What they knew and what they did "made the difference."

I have kept in touch with Mrs. Wedberg and Miss Sherman over the years and someday I must remember to ask them what sort of professional education they had—whether they learned "what to teach" or "how to teach."

These two teachers are the type called for by Randall M. Whaley of the National Academy of Sciences-National Research Council, when he told the Bowling Green Conference:

Without adequate numbers of inspiring, well-informed teachers, fully prepared to meet their responsibilities in our schools, we cannot have good education, and without good education we cannot hope for long to meet successfully the challenges of a changing world.

How do you prepare these teachers? How do you train them? How do you teach them?

It certainly is not an "either/or" question of subject matter versus professional education, said Francis V. Lloyd, Jr., superintendent of schools in Clayton, Missouri:

A great deal of time has been wasted, in my judgment, in useless bickering, and I am sorry to say that both sides have been equally guilty in running off, crying fire and bloody murder; whereas if they had remained calm and sat together around a table, they would have discovered that in most instances their aims were very similar. The real question, as it has always been since Aristotle first started dealing with students, is what is a proper balance?

Whatever a "proper balance" may be, it is not a fixed and rigid mathematical formula which specifies exactly so many semester hours of "methods" and exactly so many courses in the humanities. It is fluid and flexible, subject to change in a fast-changing and ever-changing world.

Before weighing and assessing the ingredients that make up a teacher's preparation, let us consider, as the conferees did at Bowling Green, just what a teacher must do, what he must be, what he must know.

In a "working paper" distributed to all participants before the conference began, Dean Francis C. Rosecrance of the College of Education, Wayne State University, discussed the "competences" a teacher should possesss.

Good teachers (1) know what they teach and how to teach it; (2) know the nature of the human organism, how learning takes place, and what motivates behavior; (3) know how to appraise an individual, to make an educational diagnosis, and to help persons develop in desirable fashion; (4) know how to work with small and large groups of people of varying ages; (5) know how to help people to think critically and independently; (6) know how to help people to be ever more eager to find out, to be curious, inventive, and creative; (7) know how to help people to become conscious of their own values, to examine these values, and to build for themselves values that are more satisfying to them and to society.

A teacher cannot know *what* to teach unless he has a mastery of his subject matter; he cannot know *how* to teach unless he has a mastery of the techniques. This was the agreement reached by the liberal arts scholars and the professional educators at Bowling Green, and this agreement was a measure of the success of the conference.

Rosecrance conceded the vital importance of a teacher's mastering his subject, and then he asked:

If you know your subject, does it necessarily follow that you can teach it effectively? . . . Most educationists would agree that methods courses are essential for teachers—but not to the exclusion of the basic courses in the various subject fields which the future teacher may need.

There are sincere educators, however, who really believe the statement, "If you know your subject you can teach it." They imply that no methods or skills are required of the teacher. Can anyone who knows his subject teach it to a blind person or a deaf person? Reasonable people will agree that a special skill is required in each of these cases. . . . Are not *all* students either "blind" or "deaf" toward ideas that are not in accord with their experiences? First comes the skill of helping the "blind" student to "see," and the "deaf" student to "hear." Then, there is the knowledge of how concepts are built, from which develops the skill of knowing what to teach first—the sequence of teaching or learning. Addition and subtraction must be mastered before one can perform the task of finding the square root of a number. . . . Without skill in teaching, learning is less likely to occur.

Rosecrance pointed out that a teacher must deal with students on a one-to-one basis, to know how to find out about the individual's interests, abilities, potentialities, problems, and prospects. He must also know how to deal with young people in groups of varying sizes. He must teach the content of the course, and also teach the skill of learning how to think. He must know how to encourage his students to be creative—to write poetry, to compose music, to paint and to draw, to model a figure, and even how to encourage the development of new ideas. And always he must help youth achieve some sense of values in life.

These are the essentials. These are the things a teacher must do.

What are the characteristics of a good teacher? Conference speakers named these qualities: a warm personality; an interest in and liking for children; emotional stability; better-than-average intelligence; an empathetic understanding of others; the feeling of being an active participant, not only in his community, but in his nation and his world; moral and ethical fitness; demonstrated ability to work with children; and professional interest and motivation.

But these things, what a teacher must *do* and what a teacher must *be,* are not enough. There are the things a teacher must *know.* According to Jack Allen:

The elementary-school teacher who, by definition, has responsibility for a single class during all or most of the school day is confronted with three core requirements: the natural sciences, including mathematics; the social sciences; and the humanities. Some background in each is essential if learners are to be confronted with a rounded body of cultural experiences. This requires more than a mere acquisition of bodies of factual knowledge. The teaching of certain important skills as they apply in general education to any or all three areas is also part of the responsibility. There are communication skills —reading, writing, speaking, listening—that apply to all three; critical thinking skills, especially in relation to the sciences and social sciences; number skills; spelling skills; and others.

J. Paul Reynolds said that:

One cannot teach significantly and really effectively at the senior-high-school level unless he has studied his subject matter far beyond the level he is teaching. For example, the algebra teacher needs to know calculus in order to present significantly the principles of algebra. He needs to know something of differential equations to deal with equations at a lower level. He must be projective in his treatment of the simpler mathematical phenomena. This same principle holds for all subject-matter areas taught in high school. A teacher of English grammar cannot instill in her pupils the beauty and significance of it unless she, herself, has studied and observed the beauty of grammatical structure in varieties of great literature. The teacher of American history cannot do an adequate job without an understanding of the background on which our whole political and economic developments have been based and an understanding of the backgrounds of the peoples who colonized the Western Hemisphere.

But this does not give the whole picture, either. Another conference participant, Warner G. Rice, pointed out:

It was once possible to gain considerable insight into a field of knowledge by mastering one or two well-planned introductory courses. This is certainly not now the case. College algebra and analytical geometry do not give an adequate grasp of what modern mathematics is about, or what it is capable of accomplishing; nor is the first-year course in biology or physics likely to suggest the modern range, or the objectives now possible, within these disciplines. The same conclusion can be drawn from an acquaintance with the scope of contemporary anthropology, or psychology, or—for that matter—literary criticism.

As one conference group reported,

Since research advances our knowledge of the fundamental principles of the various subjects to be taught, of how youngsters live and learn, *the education of a teacher can never stop*. The teacher must, in college and throughout his professional career, be in close contact with the scholars who are creating in their fields.

All this would seem to prove the old saying that "you can't teach what you don't know." But Margaret Mead, famed anthropologist from the American Museum of Natural History, told the conference:

Then there was a very interesting line which said, "you can't teach some-body something you don't know." Now that fascinated me, because if we can't, we had better quit right now. If we can't teach every student we've got something we don't know in some form, we haven't a hope of educating the next generation, because what they are going to need is what we don't know.

We need to teach students to think, when you don't know what method to use, about a problem which is not yet formulated.

This, then, is the teacher—the teacher who must know what he teaches, but be able to teach what he does not know; who must under-stand his pupils, be they mentally retarded or geniuses, guide them, give to them of himself, and draw from them their utmost potential.

"Always there stands the teacher . . . ," whose one and un-changing job is to enlarge the student's understanding of the universe.

CHAPTER THREE

Everybody Has to Get
into the Act

There was many an agreement reached at Bowling Green, and many a misconception (and myth-conception) laid to rest. There was, in addition, the identification of many problems that had to be faced and worked out at a later date.

The participants agreed, for instance, that prospective teachers need more and better education, that the deadwood and trivia should be cleared out of the teacher education programs, that higher standards mean more, not fewer teachers. There was agreement that knowing "how to teach" and "what to teach" are both important. And, if the conference did not come up with an ideal program of teacher education, broken down into hours and subjects, it at least exploded such myths as "methods courses take up half a student's time" and "education courses run from first to last right through the four-year cycle."

But the greatest, most vital agreement of all—because it promises so much for the future—was the virtually unanimous acknowledgment that teacher education is the responsibility of the *entire* college or university. Everybody has to get into the act. No professor, no department, can stand aloof. This theme was stressed and stressed again in group discussions, in the major conference addresses, in private talks, and in lunchtime conversations. The phrase "total college" was used so much it almost became a cliché.

Premier Georges Clemenceau of France once said, "War is too important to be left to the generals." Dean Lindley J. Stiles of the School of Education, University of Wisconsin, borrowed the thought and told the conference:

The education of teachers is too important to the nation to be left to the sole jurisdiction of any single group, whether it be composed of professors of education whose central concern has always been for teacher education or of liberal arts professors, many of whom have only recently begun to recognize a long-ignored obligation to help make policy in this area. Teacher education is properly the responsibility of the entire institution.

Participants of the Bowling Green Conference were emphatic in their conviction that if a college or university is *not* willing to make teacher education a central, and not incidental, function, then it ought to quit trying to do the job at all.

In recent years, particularly, college professors have complained bitterly about the preparation of the young men and women who come to them as freshmen: "They can't read, they can't write, they don't know basic arithmetic, their English is atrocious." If this is true, it is an indictment of their high-school teachers, and if the high-school teachers failed to learn their subject matter well enough to teach it properly, it is an indictment of the college professors. This is one of those revolving arguments that could spin on indefinitely and regardless of the rights and wrongs of it the continual hassle would not prove anything or—more important—do anything. At Bowling Green it was decided something ought to be done.

As Lawrence Kimpton said during the period when he was chancellor of the University of Chicago:

> The universities must stop grousing about the education of our high-school students and get back into the business of training teachers. The schools of education must become a real part of the universities, and the universities must begin to relate themselves properly and effectively to the work of the schools of education.[1]

There has been, in the past, a notable lack of cooperation between the academic scholars and the professional educators in the preparation of teachers. Randall M. Whaley of the National Academy of Sciences-National Research Council acknowledged this freely when he told the conference:

> For too long those of us in the academic disciplines, in the departments of sciences and humanities in our colleges and universities, have not adequately assumed our share of responsibility for educational planning. For too long, many of us have given lip service only to the special needs of prospective teachers.

Warner G. Rice, chairman of the Department of English Language and Literature, University of Michigan, pointed out that "One learns to teach partly by being well taught," and that "Every [college] course can be, in a modest way, a course in 'methods' without

[1] Lawrence A. Kimpton, "The Universities and the High Schools," in "Secondary Education Re-Examined," Francis S. Chase, editor, *School Review* 65: 50; Spring 1958.

obscuring—indeed, often with advantage to—its other objectives."

What can college professors do to improve their teaching of future teachers? The most frequently heard suggestion was that they get out into the field and learn what is going on in the high schools and the elementary schools. This applied to professors of education and to the academic professors as well. Classroom teachers repeatedly asked that college teachers of English, history, biology, and other so-called "solid subjects" visit the schools and try to understand the problems of high-school and elementary-school teachers. It also was suggested that outstanding elementary- and secondary-school teachers should be used to teach college students how to teach their subjects.

But the conference went much further than this. It asked—it demanded—that all departments of the college or university take an active hand in planning the content and the sequence of the teacher education program.

Such cooperation is not impossible; sometimes it is not even difficult. It can be seen in action at Duke University and at the University of Wisconsin, for instance. William H. Cartwright, chairman of the Department of Education at Duke, told how it works in his institution.

We . . . have a "University Committee on Public Education and the Training of Teachers." It is chaired by the chairman of the Department of Education and includes six other members. They come from the departments of chemistry, economics, English, history and mathematics. Among them are the dean of the Graduate School and the director of the summer session. The committee is advisory to the university administration and to the appropriate faculties. It keeps informed on the status of teacher education at Duke and makes recommendations on such policies and actions as it chooses or are referred to it. While it is advisory only, its advice is respected.

An example of the solving of problems through good faith rather than by drawing lines is seen in the way we have handled the so-called "special-methods" courses for prospective teachers. We have not quibbled about which department should offer these courses. We *have* insisted that the professors teaching them should know their subjects, know the schools, and have a genuine interest in public education. . . .

Not only has an academic professor taught professional work in the Department of Education, but a professor of education has taught academic courses in academic departments. Probably the cordial relations between departments have been aided by the fact that in recent years the Department of Education has added several professors who took their doctorates in fields other than education. Thus we have professors of education whose Ph.D. degrees were earned with majors in history, mathematics, psychology, and the social sciences. But the large majority of the department hold degrees in education, and there are members of the university faculty both in and out of the Department of Education who hold the Doctor of Education degree. . . .

A slightly different approach is being tried at St. Mary's College in Winona, Minnesota. Brother Julius, Dean of St. Mary's, told one of the discussion groups that the school is trying to persuade every freshman to take a course in the philosophy of education, whether or not he plans to become a teacher.

"It works both ways," Brother Julius said. "The student gets an understanding of the wonderful way in which the mind works. And it might influence some of them to become teachers."

Also at St. Mary's a real effort was made to return as many as possible of the usual professional education courses to the various academic departments concerned. Thus, the philosophy of education is now taught by the Philosophy Department, sociology of education by the Sociology Department, and psychology of education by the Psychology Department. The History Department held out for seven years, Brother Julius said, before agreeing to take over the teaching of the history of education.

One member of the discussion group pointed out that "The members of the academic departments have one real love, one main interest—their subject-matter fields. There is a risk that the Philosophy Department will concentrate on philosophy as such, and not on the philosophy of education."

One discussion group suggested the use of "liaison professors." Each academic department would appoint a faculty member to work directly with the department of education in preparing teachers in that subject area. The faculty member would share in the supervision of student teachers, serve as curriculum adviser to students in his field, be responsible for some of the instruction in teaching "methods," and initiate and encourage research in the improvement of the teaching of his particular subject matter.

Sometimes it takes drastic action to get the liberal arts department and the education department of a university together. At the Kansas Conference of 1959, Ralph E. Page, Dean of the Arts and Sciences College at the University of Florida, told the following story.

For thirty years, he said, there had been friction between the two colleges. Neither side would trust the other any further than it absolutely had to. In 1956, the president of the university issued a fiat, outlining the area of responsibility of each college. "On the basis of that fiat," Page said, "we started to make some progress. We had a road map, but we were still running two buses." A year later the president took drastic measures to halt the feuding. He called the two deans, together with their respective assistants, into a room and told them, in effect, not to come out until they had reached an agreement—but to come out soon.

It took some time to break through the ice of doubt and mistrust but, Page said:

We finally found there were no real differences of opinion. For 10 years Dean J. B. White of the College of Education and myself had been operating by remote control. The reports coming back to our central offices were exaggerated out of all proportion. Even so, we didn't really trust each other. So we spelled out an extremely comprehensive document in which we really made a treaty. I seriously doubt the Big Four Foreign Ministers ever argued more over words and their meaning. We finally decided to meet once a week. Eventually, we decided that if we were going to meet, we might as well eat together, too. After all, we couldn't get too contaminated just sitting down at the same table with the other side. Now that treaty we made isn't needed. In fact, when we wanted to bring it to this conference, we could find only one copy of it. Within a month we had set up committees in the various subject-matter fields. We told those committees to do the same thing we had done—go off somewhere and reach an agreement, and not come back until they had. In finding this road to real progress, we learned that there are three essentials to co-operation: (1) there must be mutual respect; (2) definite roles in a co-operative enterprise must be established; (3) effective channels of communication must be established. We found we hadn't been speaking the same language.

And how far did this rapport go? "In one committee," said Dean White, "we had a liberal arts man saying there should be two methods courses for the subject, and the professional education man insisting that one such course was enough."

CHAPTER FOUR

So Much to Do—So Little Time

Throughout the Bowling Green Conference—and those which followed at Lawrence, Kansas, and San Diego—there ran one main theme: Whatever may be the proper ingredients of courses and hours in a teacher's education, they cannot all be jammed into a four-year program. The teacher needs a broader and deeper education than ever before; if this means five, six, or even seven years of preparation, that is the way it will have to be. Part of this theme was the call from all concerned for much higher professional standards, with the insistence that higher standards will lure more, not fewer, capable students into the field. Time is one of the problems; this will be explained in detail in a later chapter.

In calling for more preparation, no one at Bowling Green was merely asking for more of the same. There was, in fact, a near-unanimous demand that all colleges and universities concerned with teacher preparation waste no more time before taking a long, hard, and critical look at their programs.

In the field of professional education, the institutions were asked to weed out the obsolete and out-dated courses, remove the unnecessary academic barriers which have only old age to recommend them, eliminate the repetition and redundancy, and evaluate all professional education courses in the light of what the student already knows before he is required to take them.

It was in the spirit of Bowling Green that these calls came from the professional educators as well as the academic scholars. There was, for instance, this admission by John I. Goodlad, then director of the Center for Teacher Education, University of Chicago, now professor of education and director of the University Elementary School, University of California at Los Angeles:

As something of a specialist in elementary education, I have long been embarrassed by the proliferation of courses in this most barren of educational wastelands. I readily concede the point so often made to justify the addition of still another three-hour impoverishment of the undergraduate's education: Teachers need to know something about safety education, about how to use a movie projector, and about rhythmic games for rainy days.

31

But not all of these things need to be done before the teacher begins to teach; nor do they require a three-hour course for the learning. Furthermore, most of them can be learned best on the job. Any proposed addition to the curriculum, at all levels of education, should first stand the rigorous test of whether it is more valuable than what it must necessarily replace.

There is much to be done, too, in the subject-matter fields. As Dean Kenneth S. Pitzer of the College of Chemistry, University of California, pointed out:

There are too many elementary-school teachers today who do not really understand arithmetic and thus, of course, do not like it. This rubs off on their pupils, and before we know it we have another generation of elementary-school teachers who likewise do not understand arithmetic and do not like it. Somehow this vicious circle must be broken, and I think this should be taken as one of the major challenges of the elementary-school teacher training institutions.

If the mathematics departments of the colleges and universities can come up with courses in which future elementary-school teachers *do* learn to understand arithmetic—and thus like it—Dean Pitzer's problem may be solved. But, another conference speaker pointed out, this does not mean that every elementary-school teacher should be forced to take a wide program in mathematics just to make certain he understands it. Professor Jack Allen of George Peabody College for Teachers reminded the conference participants that all such teachers need a great variety of understandings and skills.

The teaching of these understandings and skills becomes an impossible order if those responsible for the subject-matter preparation of elementary-school teachers assume that every elementary-school teacher must have a course in differential calculus or comparative anatomy or the history of the West or Milton. . . . What is really suggested, then, is that any college preparing elementary-school teachers must continually evaluate its own curriculum. Is this course really going to help the teacher of a nine-year-old? This is the kind of question that will have to be asked and answered. *Many college and university people who are crying for a better educated group of elementary-school teachers may, if they are realistic, find it necessary to admit that their own programs do not always provide a useful bill of fare.*

A survey of programs for elementary-school teachers, prepared as a "working paper" for conference participants, reported that "it is indeed very difficult, if not virtually impossible" to provide, within a four-year program, any substantial amount of all the types of subject matter currently being advocated for such teachers. Such fields as foreign languages, mathematics, and literature are generally omitted or are relatively weak, and the biological sciences do not get any great amount of attention.

What is good and necessary for the elementary-school teacher is also good and necessary for the high-school teacher, the conference participants declared. They, too, need more depth in the subject matters they will teach for, as one speaker said, "there can be no substitute for that feeling of confidence and assurance that comes from having such knowledge and understanding."

It quickly became apparent at Bowling Green that if teachers are to be properly prepared, they must have a longer period of preparation. Some discussion groups agreed that the student should first complete the four-year sequence for a bachelor's degree, and then embark on his professional training. The most oft-mentioned reasons were: (1) to provide the time necessary for an adequate, general, liberal education; (2) to provide the freedom and time which professional education needs for realistic laboratory-centered (i.e., student teaching) program of preparation; (3) to give status to the profession of teaching. On the third point, one group said, "Neither the public nor other professions will ever accept as really professional a training program which is largely undergraduate." It also was frequently mentioned that by starting the professional program *after* the four-year bachelor's degree program, the door would be left open to the many students who are late in arriving at a vocational choice. On the other hand, it also was recommended that there be some sort of counseling or other introduction to the teaching field as early as possible.

Dr. Goodlad threw some pepper into the discussion pot when he outlined to the full conference what he thought teacher education should be and do. First of all, Goodlad would have all strictly professional courses removed entirely from the first two years of the college. At the same time, he would have the study of schools and the learning processes built much more firmly into the program of general education.

The average college student is abysmally ignorant of the educational institutions of which he is a part and, later, comes to his responsibilities as a parent and taxpayer armed with a miscellany of folklore, half-truths, misconceptions, and prejudices. Worse still, in becoming a parent and taxpayer, he frequently becomes, too, a self-styled expert on child-rearing and schooling, compounding confusion by enthusiastically sharing his ignorance on a communal basis.

Goodlad also suggested that the school of education should remove itself from the undergraduate realm, becoming instead a graduate professional school. This, he said, did not mean that teacher education would become entirely a graduate function, but rather that teacher education would become a college-wide function, with responsibility for it allocated differently than at present.

"We must abandon the idea that adequate professional preparation *can* be done in the four-year college," Goodlad said. "This phase of the teacher's preparation should be regarded only as a beginning, a chance to observe, participate in, and think about his future career while still in the main channels of the educative enterprise."

The traditional "education courses" would disappear entirely from the four-year program, under the Goodlad scheme of things. Instead, prospective teachers would become teacher aides working beside a superior teacher, first for several hours a week and later for most of the day in practice-teaching experiences. This would be accompanied by intensive seminars on the function of the schools, the nature of learning, and principles of curriculum construction, and by conferences on the use of specific instructional techniques. The speaker commented that "I cannot help noting with some considerable satisfaction that what is being proposed here eliminates all the so-called special methods or special-fields courses from the preparation programs of elementary-school teachers."

After completion of the four-year college course, the prospective teacher would embark on a residency in a school, just as a young physician becomes a "resident" in a hospital. Such a residency would normally last about three years, during which time he would be under the surveillance of his senior colleagues, one or more of whom would have the responsibility of inducting him into his duties. At the conclusion of this residency, the young teacher normally would be awarded a master's degree. During this three- or four-year period he would be paid a salary roughly equivalent to that paid beginning teachers in city and suburban schools; however, upon formally "entering the profession" at the end of his term of residence, the teacher would be paid the same salary now given in those districts after ten years' service.

Goodlad acknowledged that his plan might be considered somewhat Utopian by skeptics but, he declared, "once having caught a glimpse of better vistas, we should then look to our feet to see what obstacles must be removed from the path to them."

Dr. Goodlad's suggested program of teacher education was only one of many presented to the conference and it quite naturally got a mixed reception. On two additional points, however, he got no argument:

1. . . . We must all come to realize that we are not suddenly a profession either by calling ourselves one or by including all our personnel in the membership of one or more "professional" organizations.

2. We must remove from our midst at least the most obviously bad apples whose presence devaluates the entire barrel. We tolerate in a few of our colleagues behavior so flagrant that it is obvious to community residents, who resent paying taxes for its perpetuation. We shelter some who are indolent and inept, as well as a few part-time workers who cry the loudest for full-time pay.

The conference-wide insistence that the teaching profession raise its own standards and that incompetents be weeded out ruthlessly was a fascinating sidelight to a number of laymen at Bowling Green, including this reporter. One speaker said the best way in which to get the far-above-average person into the teaching field would be a more rigorous intellectual curriculum which would make teaching "more attractive to the ambitious and bright and more formidably discouraging to the dull and apathetic."

Some proposals for an extended teacher education program did not go quite so far as Goodlad's. One discussion group, for instance, merely agreed that "At least five years of preparation shall be required before a teacher is given a certificate entitling him to *full* professional status." Another group said there should be a four-year program of basic education, with some exploration of the teaching field, followed by one to four years of professional education, including student teaching.

One idea which went a bit further was presented to a discussion group by Vern Wagner, Professor of English at Wayne State University. He proposed that all college students, including future teachers, should have four years of liberal arts, including broad and basic education in many fields of study and specialization in depth in one of them. Only then would the student begin to work seriously at the skills and knowledge that would prepare him for a vocation, a profession, or the practice of an art. In the case of teachers, Wagner said, this could mean a fifth year of college, containing the direct teacher training that is generally spread over two or three or four years, or it could be a one-year "internship" in an actual teaching position under the guidance of a master teacher.

The call for specialization in depth in a subject-matter field was echoed again and again at Bowling Green. A college dean said, "I don't want someone teaching my son chemistry if he has had only a minor in chemistry—my son would probably get his head blown off." A specialist in foreign languages declared that unless a language teacher has had real depth in the subject, his students will become "linguistic cripples" who would be better off if they never took the course. Dean Mark H. Ingraham of the University of Wisconsin, in a message to the conference, said he felt no high-school teacher should teach an academic subject without a major in that subject, and that for the last two years of high school, the teacher should have a master's degree in his field. And a committee of the American Association for the Advancement of Science (AAAS) presented a report suggesting that college students preparing to teach high-school science or mathematics should spend roughly half their time on those subjects. Only that sort of preparation seems reasonable, the committee said, if the teacher is to be properly prepared. The committee also suggested that in nearly every case the future high-school science or math teacher should plan to return to college for at least one more year after starting his career.

A complicating factor in the preparation of science and math teachers, the committee said, is that 80 to 90 per cent of them are required to teach several such courses, *not* just one. This can be worked out, it said, in such combinations as physics and math, chemistry and physics, and biology and health. But it is virtually impossible to plan a four-year program that will properly prepare a teacher in such widely divergent areas as English and physics, social science and chemistry, or physical education and mathematics. The committee proposed the following suggested courses for future high-school teachers of science and math (figures are in semester hours of college work, based on a total of 120 semester hours usually required for a degree):

Mathematics: 30 hours of math and 18 hours of supporting sciences, the latter to include physics and other courses chosen from chemistry, biology, astronomy, geology, and meteorology.

Physics: 20 to 25 hours in physics, and enough in the supporting sciences to total 60 to 62 hours. The supporting sciences were listed as chemistry, mathematics, biology, and earth science.

Chemistry: 32 hours of chemistry, 8 of physics, and 12 of mathematics.

Biology: 30 hours of biology, 12 of chemistry, 8 of physics, 6 of math, and 3 of earth science.

The committee had no formula for the preparation of a general science teacher. It noted, however, that such teachers should have a broad background in all fields of science, plus a specialty in one or more fields.

One conference speaker may have been only half-joking when he warned of an inherent danger in asking a prospective high-school physics teacher to major in physics: it would be self-defeating in these days of apparently insatiable demand by private industry for trained scientists—the prospective teacher might be lured away from the classroom.

The AAAS committee did not specify how much time it thought the prospective teacher should devote to professional education courses.

It noted, however, that such courses, as well as those in the social studies and humanities, are essential "to help give him the kind of perspective that we like the top-rate scholar and citizen to have." This was typical of the conference, and somewhat surprising to many participants and observers. The conference might easily have foundered or broken up completely in a hassle about "what to teach" versus "how to teach" if either the professional educators or the academic scholars had come to Bowling Green with chips on their shoulders, determined to fight it out on the line of courses and semester hours.

One discussion group suggested that 15-20 per cent of a prospective teacher's time in the four-year college course should be devoted to professional courses, 45-50 per cent to general education, 25 per cent to subject matter fields (specialization), and 10 per cent to free electives. Another group recommended 20 per cent in professional education, 40 per cent in general education, and 40 per cent in specialization. Otherwise—and keeping in mind the demands to weed out the obsolete and repetitious courses—the discussion groups went about the business of seeking agreements instead of fights. In particular there was a great and wonderful lack of such statements as "If you can teach, you can teach anything," and "If you know your subject well enough you can teach it to anyone."

Perhaps one good reason for this is that no one knows for sure just how much professional education a teacher needs. One conference participant declared that in 1957 General Motors Corporation spent more money just to modify the automatic transmissions on its automobiles than was spent in all the United States on educational research. This might be a hard statement to prove—or to disprove, for that matter—but certain it is that more research is needed. The official conference report noted that "We are virtually devoid of research evidence as to the relationship between the kind of preparation taken during one's four-year career as a college student and his performance later on the job as a teacher." There were specific proposals that former students now teaching be asked to evaluate their professional courses, and requests for research into the entire question of practice teaching—when it should take place, how long it should last, and so forth.

Because a teacher's education, like a woman's work, is never "done," the Bowling Green Conference inevitably turned its attention to post-graduate work open to teachers (known in the trade as the in-service program). Jack Allen painted the sometimes dismal picture with these words:

All too frequently the elementary-school teacher, returning for graduate study, is confronted with a dilemma. He would like to know more mathematics. His teaching experience tells him he needs some work in geography. The family budget also reminds him that he needs a master's degree. A sense of academic respectability causes the departments of mathematics and geography to deny the teacher courses for which he could receive graduate credit. The only realistic alternative for the teacher is to take a series of courses in "The Teaching of _____," courses usually offered in the department of education. Forthwith, of course, the unfortunate teacher is castigated for taking the easy way out. But this is not a problem which the academician can dismiss so lightly. He is not concerned with an inexperienced sophomore, but with an individual of mature purpose.

The secondary-school teacher, returning for graduate study, is confronted with somewhat different alternatives. If the undergraduate major has represented a thorough concentration in a single discipline, then the M.A. program might well be directed toward building some breadth, as well as further depth. If, by contrast, there has been good breadth in the undergraduate program, then the graduate program might well carry more emphasis on depth. All too often, however, neither direction is followed. In too many instances secondary-school teachers work in graduate programs almost entirely divorced from their areas of teaching responsibility, working in a major program labeled "Secondary Education," or even simply "Education," and ultimately obtaining a degree with little or no work in a subject-matter field. Where such situations prevail, the fault lies with the college or university, with certification provisions and, of course, with the teacher himself. *It is this kind of practice which has provided the critics of teacher education with some of their best ammunition.*

It does not *have* to be this way, as witness Dr. Cartwright's description of the "Master of Arts in Teaching" degree at Duke University: "This degree was deliberately designed to encourage high-school teachers to have more work in liberal arts. On the one hand, teachers already certified are urged to major in academic subjects. On the other, liberal arts graduates with little or no professional education may combine work toward certification and the degree by majoring in education."

There was no audible argument with the theory advanced by several conference speakers that there comes a time in every teacher's life when he can continue teaching without the necessity of taking further courses in professional education. John R. Beery, Dean of the School of Education, University of Miami, states the case:

Other professions, such as law and medicine, also face changing conditions and new discoveries that are important in the professional work of the practitioner. However, these people are not required by law to take refresher work. Professional pride is considered sufficient motivation to keep up to date. Should there not also come a time in the teacher's professional career, say at the master's degree level, when he is considered to be a full-fledged member of a profession and his continuing professional growth can be safely left to him?

The "requirement by law" which Beery mentioned is a reference to certification, one of the thorniest problems in the entire picture of teacher education. The teacher has nothing to say about certification, but it prescribes the courses he shall take and the graduate studies he shall pursue. The department or college of education often has little to say about it, but it molds and shapes the curriculum it must offer.

A certificate is nothing more nor less than a license to teach. The license is granted in each of the fifty states by the state board of education, in many states, upon the recommendation of the college of education, but strictly in accordance with the rules the board has laid down: so many semester hours of this, so many semester hours of that. Many states require that a teacher, to keep his certificate up-to-date, must go back to school and take a certain number of courses every so many years.

Now, all this sounds logical—and it ought to be logical, but in all too many cases it is not. So, while the conference delegates did not go to Bowling Green to discuss certification, they could not really avoid it; teacher education results in certification, and certification is one of the marks of professional status.

The core of the problem is that each individual state board of education has its own ideas of what properly belongs in teacher-education programs, and it quite often bears no resemblance to what the board in a neighboring state might think. One state may require 12 semester hours of professional education for a high-school teacher, and another 27. One state may require a foreign language teacher to have 12 semester hours in that language; another may demand 48 semester hours. To further complicate the picture, there is no similarity in the numbers and types of certificates the various states might issue: there are 65 separate certificates in New Jersey, three in Virginia. There is confusion, too, on specific courses. As one of the conference working papers pointed out, "The psychology of education (required in most states) seems to be what any particular instructor of this subject thinks it is. This same observation can be made regarding methods of instruction and even practice teaching."

All this hodge-podge might be excusable if certification were doing the job it was cut out to do—provide only the best teachers for each state. But it does not. A topnotch teacher, with just the sort of professional, general, and specific education that a good teacher should have, and with years of experience, can move across a state line and find himself unable to secure a teaching position because he had one type of course instead of another. In this situation, of course, there is usually the escape hatch of a temporary or emergency certificate. But this has been so rudely abused that most educators would like to see it abolished completely. Consider the words of Dean Pitzer of California:

In many states there are now loopholes in the certification requirements which allow the assignment of teachers to subjects in which they are completely unprepared. In my own state this is no loophole, it is a wide open boulevard since it is quite legal to assign a teacher with a general secondary [high-school] credential to a subject in which he has had no preparation whatsoever. I hasten to add that I do not believe this is being done willfully, but a study by the California Teachers Association showed that teacher-shortage conditions were forcing such assignments on unprepared teachers at an alarmingly high frequency. Only half the teachers of English, science, and mathematics classes have a major in the subject taught, and only about half of the remaining teachers have even a minor.

Small wonder, then, that there was a call at Bowling Green for a master plan of certification. William P. Viall, of the New York State Education Department, told the conference:

A state-by-state approach to certification standards, generation after generation, in this country is neither economical nor sensible. . . . It is true that, constitutionally, education is the responsibility of the states. But these times of ours are different from those in which any generation has ever lived before. The growth and mobility of population, shifts in economic areas, the sudden and welcome public interest in school programs to meet the needs of a scientific age call for an approach to certification problems with the nation as a whole in view.

Perhaps the most important agreement reached at Bowling Green on the question of certification was that the teaching profession should assume its rightful role in determining the standards for certification. This could not properly be called a revolt, but a request that the profession be allowed to assume some of the responsibility for the licensing of its own practitioners, just as doctors and dentists and lawyers assume the responsibility in their own state boards.

There was much talk of certification at Bowling Green, and there was a precedent-shattering action taken, too. The National Association of State Directors of Teacher Education and Certification (NASDTEC) came out flatly and strongly for reciprocity among the states. Under terms of a unanimous agreement reached by representatives of thirty-five states participating in the Bowling Green meeting, the teacher who has been graduated by an institution fully accredited by the National Council for Accreditation of Teacher Education

(NCATE) would be eligible to take a teaching post in any state, even if the certification standards of that state differ from his own. This, of course, was only a statement of position, but it promised long-overdue action and effort at the state level. Under the agreement the NCATE, a voluntary accrediting agency created by the profession in 1952, becomes "the last word" on the subject. In 1960, some twenty states had adopted the above provision to speed reciprocity in teacher certification.

So important did the Bowling Green planners and sponsors consider the question of certification that an entire conference, to be held in San Diego in 1960, was scheduled to deal with it and the twin problem of accreditation.

A number of issues dealing with teacher education were identified and discussed but in no way settled at Bowling Green: How do you educate the superior teacher needed for superior students? How can you insure that all the skills needed by a teacher can be taught, without building a separate course around each one of them? How much more professional education is required for an elementary-school teacher than for a high-school teacher? Which things should be formally organized into classes, and which things should a teacher learn as he goes along, or in practice teaching?

This, perhaps, is as it should be. Certainly there was no thought that the Bowling Green Conference was going to settle all the problems of today, and of the day after tomorrow as well. It may be that those problems cannot be solved permanently, anyway. Ralph W. Tyler, director of the Center for Advanced Study in Behavioral Sciences at Palo Alto, California, pointed out:

. . . changing conditions in which . . . students will be living, our growing knowledge of the conditions which promote learning, our growing knowledge of social psychology, of various cultures and subcultures in our cities and rural areas—all these developments require restudy and continued collaborative effort. *I do not expect in our lifetime that the task of building the curriculum and developing high-quality teaching will be completed.*

But Bowling Green was a start.

CHAPTER FIVE

The Bed of Procrustes

Once upon a time, according to some of the most reliable sources in mythology, weary travelers in Eleusis used to stop at the house of Procrustes and ask for a night's lodging. Procrustes would show them to the guest room and measure them against the size of the bed. If the bed was too short, the guests were chopped down to size; if the bed was too long, the guests were stretched until they fit. In either case, alas, the "fitting" usually was fatal.

Now Procrustes' unique form of hospitality and the concerns of the 1,025 delegates to the Kansas Conference seem far removed; yet, they did have something in common—the problem of "making it fit."

At Bowling Green the year before, the liberal arts scholars and the professional educators had found, to their happy astonishment, that they could agree on generalities: teacher education must be improved; a teacher must know *how* to teach as well as *what* to teach; the education of teachers must be the responsibility of all departments of the college or university.

Now they had been given a fearsome assignment: work out an ideal, four-year teacher education program including the proper amounts of general or "liberal" education, specialization in a subject-matter field, and professional or "how-to-teach" courses. They not only did not do their assignment, they decided not even to try. They agreed that "ideal" and "four-year" were incompatible terms in a discussion of something as complex as teacher education. The knowledge and the skills that today's (and tomorrow's) teachers need cannot be crammed into four short years of college—and this is education's Bed of Procrustes. It is true that the source of 90-95 per cent of all our teachers is a four-year program, but this does not make it the proper source and certainly it does not make it ideal. Besides, it was obvious to the delegates that no strict hour-and-course formula for teacher education could be found that could or would be adopted by all the 1,147 teacher-education institutions in the country.

There may have been a temptation to do a little horse-trading at the Kansas Conference, to swap a course in "methods" for a course in "general education" and come up with a program that everyone could accept, even if they did not particularly like it. If the temptation was there, the participants seem to have resisted it, and they did not—at least very often—try to take all the scattered parts of education and build them into a teacher. What they tried to do, and with considerable success, was to decide what a teacher should be and then find the parts that fit the picture. There were, indeed, some basic agreements on courses and even on percentages, but these were more general than specific.

If the Kansas Conference failed to come up with a detailed picture of just what teacher education should be, at least some of the pieces started falling into place. There was, for instance, fairly general agreement on these points:

1. All schools and departments in a university or college must share in the responsibility for teacher education.

2. There must be early identification of prospective teachers, selective recruitment-and-admission standards, and effective guidance policies—this means weeding out the incompetent as well as attracting the most able.

3. A fifth year in college for teachers is becoming a "must," although that fifth year might follow actual teaching experience.

4. A substantial part of the total program must be devoted to general education, including the humanities, social science, and mathematics.

5. All teachers, elementary- and secondary-school, need a substantial amount of academic specialization in one particular field.

6. Elementary-school teachers need more courses in methods than do those preparing for high-school posts.

It would be nice to report that all this was accomplished in a spirit of sweetness and brotherly love; nice, but hardly accurate. Harsh words were spoken and sore toes were trod upon. There was little if any bitterness, but there was considerable blunt talk. There was, for instance, the high-school teacher who looked the college dean squarely in the eye and declared, "I couldn't possibly disagree more with practically everything you have said." (What he had said was that bachelor's degrees in education should be abolished, school administration should be eliminated as a major field of study, and teachers' salaries should be "de-mechanized"—in other words, that a mathematics teacher should be paid more than an English teacher.)

Then there was the newspaperman covering the conference who summed up his impressions after the third day in this way:

If there is anything certain in the uncertain world of education it seems to be this—America's teachers of the future are going to spend less time learning *how* to teach and more time learning *what* to teach.

When the story appeared the next morning in the *Daily Reporter,* the conference newspaper distributed to all participants, there were outraged wails of anguish from a group of dissenters.

Perhaps the reporter had been caught with his biases showing. Perhaps he had over-generalized. Perhaps he was dead wrong. Still and all, there was a very great deal of discussion of professional education and many of the comments were something less than flattering. It was not so much that the courses were wrong in themselves, just that there were too many of them. This is a hassle that has been going on for years, and it is not likely to end soon.

Consider, if you will, the comments of Eugene E. Slaughter, an English professor at Southeastern Oklahoma State College:

> Colleges and universities which complain that their students can't speak or write good English have only themselves to blame. . . . The great majority of our grade- and high-school teachers were not properly prepared for their jobs in college . . . and they can't pass on to their students what they don't know themselves. Some of our colleges and universities insist that a student spend half his time on professional education courses, . . . and others permit it. This is completely out of balance. Such institutions think it's enough to know how to teach, whether or not you know anything about what to teach.

Dean Harold L. Clapp of the Division of Language and Literature, Grinnell (Iowa) College, and vice-president of the Council for Basic Education, acknowledged that professional education, when it is rigorous and disciplined, can appreciably increase a teacher's perception and effectiveness. He thought, however, that the "technical training" of teachers might well be done "with the equivalent of about three beefed-up courses incorporating the pertinent aspects of psychology and educational history and philosophy, including something of the history of the curriculum. I would no doubt expect students to do a bit of reading on their own in some of the areas neglected in the courses—notably the whole know-how aspect of teaching, the bag-of-tricks side of things: the care and feeding of the bulletin board and the like."

Sister Mary Emil, I.H.M., executive secretary of the Sister-Formation Conference, National Catholic Educational Association, suggested that all the ingredients of professional education could be drawn together into two courses. Dean Werner A. Baum of the Graduate School, Florida State University, told the conference:

> I would certainly not permit the undergraduate to take such courses as—and I quote a reasonably typical example from the catalog of my own institution—"The School in Community Life," which purports "to develop

an outlook and point of view which will enable the school to render service to the community" and carries as much credit as educational psychology.

G. Baley Price, chairman of the mathematics department of the University of Kansas, declared, "it is well known that many students do not like the education courses they are required to take" and "many good students are repelled by them."

There is not very much that is new and original about these comments—the liberal arts scholars have been saying them for some time, and oftentimes a good deal more pungently. So there was a note of freshness to the comments of Ewald Turner, a junior-high-school teacher in Pendleton, Oregon, who came to the conference as president of the NEA's Department of Classroom Teachers. Turner reported on a personal survey he had made:

A number of teachers at the elementary-school level protested the necessity of taking numerous methods courses. They feel that the methods of good teaching are essentially and basically the same, whether they are used in social studies, arithmetic or the language class. They strongly supported a general course in methods of teaching, rather than a methods course for each individual subject-matter area.

So here we are, beating the professional educators about the head and shoulders and ridiculing their courses in methods. And this is most unjust. It has been going on so long that much of the criticism stems from habit, rather than from a real knowledge of what is going on. As a political scientist told the Kansas Conference:

One of the cherished fringe benefits of any faculty of a college of liberal arts . . . is that of freely casting unwarranted, uninformed, and nonsensical aspersions upon the ancestors, the progeny, the intent, and the capabilities of the faculties and programs of the professional schools.

Gertrude Stein tells us that a rose is always a rose; the same is not true of methods courses. At Central Missouri State College, for instance, there is a course called "Problems in Teaching Elementary Mathematics." On the face of it, this sounds like an out-and-out methods course. However, the course is aimed primarily at broadening the prospective teacher's understanding of mathematics and is, therefore, essentially a subject-matter course. It was said at Bowling Green, and repeated at Kansas, that too many elementary-school teachers do not understand mathematics, therefore do not like it, and as a result pass their dislike on to their students. This particular "methods" course at Central Missouri State College is designed to counteract that mis-understanding and dislike, and it is a course that the academic schol-ars should approve. Similar courses are offered in science, music, and art, combining solid background in those subjects with teaching techniques.

The suggestion that two or more professional education courses could be combined into one implies that this is not being done now —but it is. At George Peabody College for Teachers three separate courses—principles of secondary education, high-school curriculum, and methods of teaching—were combined into a single course called "high-school teaching and curriculum."

These are just two examples of the way that professional educators are trying to streamline and strengthen their programs. Similar de-velopments have been going on in other schools. There may be a long way yet to go, but the journey is under way.

Professional courses were not the only aspect of teacher preparation that were criticized by educators. Said one college dean: "If there is anything damming up the progress of education, it is the prolifera-tion of courses. And this does not just apply to education courses. It would take you four years just to take all the courses offered in the English Department." Another remarked that he had taken forty semester hours of history in college and had learned more about George Washington than he really cared to know. This business of piling one course on top of another in the various university or col-lege departments is not the result of conscientious professors trying to meet the honest needs of their students. To the contrary, all too often it is the result of a professor's all-consuming interest in some partic-ular area of his field. If he has a passionate interest in Confederate money, for example, it may turn up as a full course in economics or history in the next catalog. This is a sin of which both the profes-sional educators and the scholars are guilty.

Participants in the Kansas Conference were divided into sixty-four separate groups and asked to invent, design, or patch together a teacher education program. Each group represented a cross-section of all the various fields interested in teacher education; thus there were few groups that reached a unanimous agreement on anything. Here, in brief, are some of the recommendations the groups made.

Professional Education

On the basis of a four-year program of 120 semester hours of study, the suggested range of professional education courses for prospective elementary-school teachers ran from 24 to 40 hours; the most frequently mentioned figure was 30. For secondary-school teachers, the range was from 15 to 30, but most of the recommendations were for 18-24 hours. Most of the participants seemed to take it for granted that elementary-school teachers need more professional courses than the secondary-school teachers—they have to teach many more subjects to relatively immature pupils; also there is a cluster of programs for elementary-school teachers that are both how-to and what-to courses. One brave soul asked that a ceiling be placed on the amount of professional education a prospective teacher would be allowed to take. "Since so many of our colleges *permit* a student to add elective work in professional education to the point that it becomes absurd," he said, ". . . I respectfully suggest a maximum of 25 per cent of work for secondary-school teachers and 35 per cent for elementary-school teachers." This idea, if adopted nation-wide, might well cut criticism of professional education by 50 per cent. It is important to note that only about half of the groups made specific suggestions about the number of hours of professional education which should be prescribed. The others apparently thought it best to treat teacher education as a whole, and let the various institutions deal with the specifics.

Only one group went so far as to specify a program by courses and hours. Other groups might argue about the content, but at least the hours fit into the generally accepted pattern:

| | Semester Hours | |
Courses	Elementary	Secondary
Orientation to the Profession	1	1
Psychological Foundations	6	6
Sociological Foundations	3	3
Method, Material, Curriculum	10	3
Observation and Student Teaching	8	8
	28	21

Student teaching was unanimously endorsed by the groups, although they did not always agree on what they wanted. One group said student teaching was "one of the softest spots in the total program." Comments and ideas about student teaching will be dealt with in a separate chapter.

General Education

When it came to mapping out a program of general education for prospective teachers, the discussion groups found themselves with a very slippery problem, indeed. Most agreed that a "general education" was a "liberal education," and that a liberal education was something that every educated person ought to have, regardless of vocational or professional aims and aspirations. It has been described as an education which is undertaken for the sheer thrill of learning, without any regard to "What good will this do me?" or "How can I use this in my job?" It could include, among other things, philosophy, a foreign language, mathematics, English, science, literature, psychology, history, political science, economics, sociology, the fine arts, music, and anthropology. The question the discussion groups found hard to answer was, "When are these subjects general education, when are they professional education, and when are they specialized education in a student's field of academic interest?"

The discussion groups seemed to agree that a substantial portion of a student's college course should be devoted to general education. The proportions ranged from 25 to 60 per cent—and the wide variance here reflected the difference in definitions. To over-simplify: Is psychology a professional course because every teacher must know something about it, or is it general education because *all* educated people must know something about it? Is a foreign language part of a liberal education, or is it part of the field of specialized knowledge that an English teacher should have? Many of the group reports expressed concern for the importance of English in the teacher education program. Two of those reports illustrate the problem mentioned above:

All teachers must accept responsibility to see that their students speak well and write well. Demonstrated competence in the use of English should be a part of the general education program of each college student.

Although a majority vote indicated that the study of a foreign language is essential to the general education of a teacher, a minority indicated that, more important, the use of English—reading, writing, and speaking—should be basic to the profession of teaching.

There seemed to be little disagreement with the idea that most of a student's first two years in college should be devoted to general education.

Specialized Education

If "you can't teach what you don't know," as many insist, then "how much do you have to know about what you're going to teach before you can teach it?" It all depends—it depends upon whether you are going to teach in elementary school or high school. If in high school, it depends upon what you are going to teach. If in elementary school, it depends upon your own particular interests, and how much specialization you can squeeze into your program.

The conferees at the Kansas Conference found it easy to agree that all prospective teachers should have education in depth, even those going into the elementary schools. Beyond that general statement they tended to bog down on the details. As far as secondary-school teachers are concerned, it is probably safe to say that most of the discussion groups favored somewhere between 40 and 60 semester hours of work in the student's "major." One group called for 30 per cent of the total four-year program in general education, 50 per cent in the field of specialization and related fields, and 20 per cent in professional education. Another said the student should complete at least one academic major (presumably about 40 hours) and, as soon as possible, work toward a second major. Because the requirements for secondary-school teachers vary with the subject to be taught, this will be taken up in more detail in Chapter Seven.

Trying to squeeze education in depth into the elementary-school teacher's four-year program is like trying to put the toothpaste back into the tube—there is just no way to make it fit. The basic problem is lack of time. By the time the student has had a basic grounding in general education, and has learned all the skills and the methods and the psychology he needs, and has dipped deeply into child growth and development, his 120 semester hours have been virtually expended. One group suggested that instead of the division into general and specialized education, 25 per cent of the elementary-school teacher's program should be devoted to professional education, with the balance devoted to courses in the liberal arts and sciences. Another group proposed that 40 per cent of the four-year program should be in elementary education with some specialization in a particular field of interest. The suggestion was made several times (and sometimes vigorously opposed) that the elementary-school teacher should work toward a major (40 hours) in an academic field—but no one went on record with the proposal that general education or professional education be trimmed down to make room for it. It was in this area particularly that the conferees found their four-year program becoming virtually a five-year program.

Foreign Languages

As if the Bed of Procrustes was not already over-crowded, the Kansas Conference participants found themselves wondering how they could squeeze more foreign language study into the teacher education program. In a major conference address Chancellor Franklin D. Murphy of the University of Kansas, now chancellor, University of California at Los Angeles, posed the question this way:

Will we have curricular patterns and educational philosophies which are geared to the realities of today and tomorrow rather than problems and issues of a generation past?

. . .

In the face of the complex and subtle problems of our day, why can we not get a greater intellectual component into our educational system to balance to some reasonable degree the high vocational orientation?

. . .

What about the tragic inarticulateness of the American people, only a few hours away from their neighbors of many languages and many proud cultures? How can any educator say that he is in the business of preparing American youth for the 20th century when he regards the study of foreign languages in his school or school system as "something extra"—something to be "stuck on" as it were? It has become popular at least to talk about foreign language study these days, and the popularity was finally made official when the federal government created a program in this field. Yet, how many of our elementary schools are actually introducing the study of foreign languages? You know the sad answer to this question as well as I. What is the enrollment in our teacher education institutions of those who would become teachers of foreign languages as compared to other fields? You know the sad answer to this question, too.

The recommendations of the discussion groups fell into three categories: most thought it would be a fine thing if all college graduates attained a mastery of a foreign language; the majority would *not* require it of all prospective teachers; and a few urged that it be required of every person receiving a college degree. One of the latter groups specified this mastery: (1) the ability to understand the foreign language when spoken at an average rate of speed by a native speaker; (2) the ability to respond intelligently in a reasonable conversational situation; and (3) the ability to read materials of moderate difficulty in the general areas of human knowledge. One group acknowledged the added burden in hours of credit and months of time that such mastery would involve, but it urged teacher education institutions to encourage it. The suggestion also was made that students majoring in foreign languages be recruited into the teaching profession. Here again, as so often at the Kansas Conference, it was a question of "making it fit."

Select and Reject

Perhaps the professional educators ought to follow the example of their colleagues in the athletic department. If there is a promising athlete—say a basketball or football star—in the smallest crossroads hamlet, the coaches will hear about him and do their best to get him to enroll at their university or college. If he fails to meet their expectations, he is reluctantly dropped from the squad but encouraged to continue his education and to get his degree. Why should not the same recruiting standards be applied to promising prospective teachers?

Participants in the Kansas Conference devoted considerable time and discussion to the early identification of good teachers, admission to the school or department of education, guidance programs, and elimination of the incompetents. It was obvious to all that the sooner a good teaching prospect is identified, the better job can be done in planning his program. Some thought identification and admission ought to start as soon as possible—as early as the freshman year and not later than the junior year. There also was the suggestion that some sort of teacher education program be devised for those who decide they want to go into teaching only after they have earned their bachelor's degrees. Several of the discussion groups urged that higher standards be established in order to encourage the able and to discourage the incompetent. One group in particular approved the practice of requiring education students to maintain a higher grade-point average than that required for the student body as a whole. Other proposals were that students be given an opportunity, early in college life, to observe the teaching process in either elementary or secondary schools, that teachers from these schools be used as counselors, and that college teachers in the liberal arts could help by encouraging good students to go into the teaching profession.

In view of the teacher shortage, perhaps the greatest shock to this reporter—at both Bowling Green and Kansas—was the insistence by the teaching profession that those who cannot teach, and teach well, be weeded out of the program before they get their certificates.

The State TEPS Chairmen, in a separate meeting at the Kansas Conference, urged that a comprehensive research study be started that would set a sort of national standard for competent teachers. Such a study would help determine what a teacher education program should be, and what type of person should be recruited into teaching. Over the past 20 years there have been many studies on the question of evaluating teaching, but, as one state chairman said, "No one has ever pulled these things together. No one has ever tried to determine a national standard. That's our big problem."

Mrs. Betty Lou Pagel of the Cheyenne, Wyoming, public schools, declared:

There is a level of competence below which no one should be allowed in a classroom. There are incompetents in every field. An incompetent plumber may flood your basement. An incompetent mechanic may ruin your car. But an incompetent teacher can ruin the education of thousands of children.

The discussion groups went along with the idea wholeheartedly. Sample comments:

The guidance process has the obligation to recognize students who are improperly or wrongly motivated or who have no motivation at all; such students might be culled from the ranks before they get to their senior year.

.   .   .

While some students will not be eliminated from the program of teacher education until they are enrolled in student teaching, the *goal* should be to deny such enrollment until there is reasonable assurance of probable success.

John B. Whitelaw of the U. S. Office of Education said the student teaching program should be the checkpoint which makes or breaks the prospective teacher. "From that point on," he declared, "there should be no question that if a student doesn't measure up well during student teaching, he is through."

Now this is a laudable idea, but it is not as easy as it might sound. How do you measure a teacher? Certainly not by adding up courses and hours and dividing by grades, although all those are factors. As Arthur Corey of the California Teachers Association pointed out:

The struggle to build a "science" of education has borne some bitter fruit. Certain quantitative aspects of teaching and learning have been isolated, instruments devised for their measurement, and symbols selected for their representation; and formulae are now being used as argument that quality in teaching can be measured quantitatively. A rose can be measured and weighed, but none would maintain that these quantitative elements, accurate as they might be, adequately measure the quality of the rose.

Corey also suggested that schools of education put their own houses in order while going about the business of judging prospective teachers:

Almost none of us teaches as well as he knows how to teach. Many of our public-school teachers feel that education professors, in spite of bad precedents set by other disciplines, should be selected for their mastery of teaching. Many teachers believe that the quality of all teaching in teacher education institutions is on the average below that in the public high schools. Those of us who teach teachers can go home and teach them better.

.   .   .

The most devastating criticism which comes from those who now teach in the public schools . . . is that there is all too little inspiration in teacher education. Here is a profession whose competence may tip the balance of our civilization and we stolidly move along with the preparation of its replacement with less excitement and sense of urgency than is exhibited by our brethren in the schools of veterinary medicine.

CHAPTER SIX

"If I Had My Way. . . ."

Liberal arts scholars, professional educators, classroom teachers, and school superintendents were given a chance at the Kansas Conference to say exactly what teacher education programs would be —if they had their way. They were told to let their imaginations run wild but to keep their proposals within the bounds of what was feasible and attainable. (These paradoxical instructions call to mind a song my father used to sing: "Mother, may I go out to swim? Yes, my darling daughter. Hang your clothes on a hickory limb—but don't go near the water.") Here are the highlights from the "If I Had My Way" presentations.

JOHN F. LATIMER, ASSISTANT DEAN OF FACULTIES, THE GEORGE WASHINGTON UNIVERSITY:

. . . It is more important for a prospective elementary- or secondary-school teacher to be well grounded in basic subjects than for any other member of our society. We cannot afford to let their high-school ground lie fallow on the mistaken notion that renewal of cultivation in college will produce the needed bountiful crop. . . .

What then should our prospective but unsuspecting teacher study in high school? The most important subject, of course, is English. What one subject is studied by more students for a longer period of time than any other? English. What one subject is hated, despised, and rejected by more students than any other? English. If we do not restore English to its rightful place in the curriculum, we make it doubly difficult, if not impossible, for our students to study and learn mathematics, science, history, foreign languages, and the rest. Unless they read, how will they study? Unless they study, how will they learn? Unless they learn, how will they teach? Or will they?

. . .

With a thorough grounding in the basic disciplines [English, a foreign language, mathematics, history and government, and science], our student now goes to college. By this time he may know that he wants to teach mathematics or English in high school. If I had my way, he would major in the given discipline and build around the major a related and logical whole. No professional courses would be permitted until he began practice teaching. . . .

Since elementary-school teachers need a broad education in several disciplines, they should major not in a single subject but in related disciplines. These could be foreign languages, a foreign language and English, sciences, or a science and mathematics, history and government. Such a grouping as this would call for some farsighted planning. It would call for a new look at our traditional teaching pattern in the elementary schools and for a new approach to curriculum planning in college. . . .

There are many subjects and many studies, but there are some without which life in the modern world would be inconceivable. It is no accident that the hard core of these subjects is the same in all civilized countries. The logic of mathematics, the laws of science, the lessons of history and principles of government are the same, no matter in what language they are written. Native tongues differ, but each is a gateway to its own procreation of culture, thought, and communication. Foreign languages differ, but they constitute the media for the transmission of ideas and the cross-fertilization of cultures.

* * *

SISTER MARY EMIL, I.H.M., EXECUTIVE SECRETARY, SISTER FORMATION CONFERENCE, NATIONAL CATHOLIC EDUCATIONAL ASSOCIATION:

If it should be that the making of a basically educated teacher would not all fit in the traditional four years, then we would plan for that right from the beginning and we would be very careful about priorities. . . .

If I had my way, the first question we would ask is not "How much professional education dare we insist on?" Nor is it "How much of an academic major can I carve out of a 120-hour curriculum?" The first question is "What is the body of intellectual habits, information, and skills which will enable this person to share in our cultural heritage in the pre-eminent way that a teacher should?" . . .

General education for prospective teachers will be the same for elementary and secondary candidates. In addition to the customary branches, it will include a foreign language or two, used within the curriculum. It will incorporate a strong grounding in the main branches of psychology. All the major social sciences will be at least introduced.

.   .   .

We will ask of the professional educator, first, that he take note of what the behavioral sciences, history, and philosophy already studied have contributed to what the young teacher should know about children, schools, society, knowledge, learning, and teaching, and we will ask him to pull all this together and to fill in what may be lacking in a single course, to be given in the last year of the program. Then we will ask some persons in the field—practicing supervisors and practicing teachers—to identify the student-teaching experiences and the acquaintance with curriculum and curricular materials which the neophyte must and can absorb before entering the classroom, and we will organize these into another course.

If general education receives the attention it deserves, if professional education is awarded the hours needed to make the first years of teaching profitable for teacher and children, and if there is a beginning of an academic specialization, time will surely run out in the first four years of college.

*   *   *

R. FREEMAN BUTTS, WILLIAM F. RUSSELL PROFESSOR IN THE FOUNDATIONS OF EDUCATION, TEACHERS COLLEGE, COLUMBIA UNIVERSITY:

But what would the undergraduate education of teachers be like if I had my way? It would consist of three main ingredients . . . :

1. *A broad education in the liberal arts and sciences.* . . . Without such liberal education the teacher will be a second-class citizen, a second-class professional, and a second-class person. This general education should begin in the freshman year and continue throughout the college preparation of the teacher. It should comprise about one-half of the total four years of undergraduate study and should continue into graduate study.

2. *Scholarly competence in a major field of learning.* Every elementary- and secondary-school teacher should undertake special study in depth and achieve a high degree of scholarly competence in some major field of learning. . . . The study of the major field should begin early in the college career and continue throughout the four years. It should comprise about one-fourth of the total four years of study and should continue into the graduate years.

3. *Professional competence in education.* Deliberate study of educa-

tion as a profession is necessary for those who would be well-qualified teachers at the outset of their careers and who would continue to grow in professional stature. This study should comprise approximately one-fourth of the total four years of study and should continue into the graduate years.

. . .

Supervised professional experience . . . should include observation, participation, student teaching, and competence in the methods of teaching and use of instructional materials. This aspect should comprise about one-half of the professional education.

. . .

Elementary-school teachers and secondary-school teachers should not be segregated into different types of institutions but should be prepared in the same multi-purpose institutions of university-level standard. Both should have similar preparation in the liberal arts and sciences and in the foundations of education. Elementary-school teachers should have a broader academic background and may not require as much specialization in a single major field of learning as do secondary-school teachers.

* * *

HAROLD L. CLAPP, HEAD, DIVISION OF LANGUAGE
AND LITERATURE, GRINNELL COLLEGE, IOWA:

If I had my way, all teachers would be wise, resourceful, humanely educated men and women with well-furnished and disciplined minds, with clear scholarly competence in some one area of the liberal curriculum, with an irresistible zeal for setting young minds on fire to the limits of individual combustibility. Now it may well be that the Good Lord has not created enough people of this kind to go around in our classrooms. If not, the problem that presents itself is (1) how to entice into the teaching profession the largest possible number of the extant potential great teachers, and (2) how to place them most strategically. . . .

Let us give teachers the best possible traditional liberal education [which] . . . implies a rigorous, demanding program beyond the capacity of the mediocre mind. The kind of teachers that I want to attract would *be* attracted. Those whom it would deter, I would be quite happy to see eased into some other calling. In this exacting four-year liberal arts program, the component that goes under the heading of "general education" would consist of a firmly rationalized

selection of things, not an I-cover-the-waterfront smattering of as
many things as possible. For example, it would give students a
meaningful look at the substance and method of one or two sciences,
not a hop-skip-and-jump "survey" of a half-dozen assorted sciences.
It would establish a high standard of knowledge of history and literacy
in English, and—for all—would make substantial inroads on some
one foreign language and culture. It would find time for these
things by tightening and condensing, by squeezing out the water of
first aid, home economics, industrial arts, and other such items that
I have been startled to find masquerading as "general education"
in certain teachers college catalogs. In short, I would substitute
discriminating selectivity for scattershot superficiality, demand depth
even in a program of breadth.

I would require of every teacher of every subject, at every level
from the kindergarten on, a full-scale, undiluted, "honest-injun"
major in one of the central disciplines of the liberal curriculum.
Away with the so-called "broad-area major," which refuses the right
to major in chemistry or physics or biology and insists instead on
elementary work in all of these plus a couple of other sciences for
bad measure. . . .

I would also, and probably first of all, throw out what seems to be
the standard substitute for a college major for elementary-school
teachers. I have searched in vain through the catalogs of a score
of Midwestern state teachers colleges for the mere *possibility*—to
say nothing of the requirement—of a genuine major for those who
are to teach in elementary schools. What I have found universally,
instead, is a dismal array of one-, two-, and three-hour courses in
art for the artless, biology for babes, chemistry for kiddies, math
and music for moppets, along with such academic fantasies as "Creative
Experiences with Materials"—which is to say, cutting and pasting for
college credit.

.   .   .

Without a tough, intellectually exacting major requirement for
all, we fail to challenge the able. Conversely, many persons must
slip into the profession who would not be able to survive the serious
upper reaches of undergraduate study. . . . Scattershot scholarship
caters to the mediocre teachers and fosters a Gresham's law by which
weak teachers drive out strong ones. . . .

I would of course do away with the "teaching minor" as normally
conceived, on the simple ground that minor competence to teach
is not good enough. I would certify no one to teach a high-school
subject in which he has had less than four years of college work,
say 24 or more semester hours.

* * *

EWALD TURNER, JUNIOR-HIGH-SCHOOL TEACHER AND PRESI-
DENT, 1958-59, NEA DEPARTMENT OF CLASSROOM TEACHERS:

(Mr. Turner reported on a personal survey of classroom teachers
he had made during his travels as president of the Department of
Classroom Teachers.)

. . . One of the most frequent suggestions made by classroom
teachers for the improvement of the teacher education program is to
acquaint prospective teachers with teaching earlier in their program.
They feel that many of the now-required education courses would be
much more meaningful after the teacher candidate has had some opportunity to observe children and to observe a qualified and capable
teacher as he works with those children.

. . .

Classroom teachers are agreed that courses in how to teach are
absolutely necessary. But when they are asked about the courses in
methods that they were required to take, they will often state that
some of the most ineffective methods of teaching were used in teaching
those courses. . . . Those who teach teachers how to teach [should]
have had successful public-school teaching experience themselves.
It is one thing to tell how it should be done from the text and
quite another when you step into a classroom of 20 to 40 elementary
or secondary students.

A number of teachers at the elementary level protested the necessity
of taking numerous methods courses. They feel the methods of
good teaching are essentially and basically the same, whether they
are used in social studies, arithmetic, or the language class. They
strongly supported a general course in methods of teaching rather
than a methods course for each individual subject-matter area. . . .
Classroom teachers . . . urge that the teacher education program
include more material that will aid them in knowing, identifying,
and understanding children. They want to know what makes them
behave the way they do and how they can better meet the special
needs of some children. They also want to know what tools and
techniques should be available once the needs of the child have been
determined.

. . .

Classroom teachers insist upon the mastery of the subject matter
by those who would be teachers. They recognize that as teachers
it will be necessary for them to be highly skilled in the chosen areas

they will teach. Elementary-school teachers tell me that this emphasis
on skill in the subject-matter area is sometimes neglected. They
point out that it is difficult for the elementary-school teacher to
establish a good foundation for any subject with the students if the
teacher is not sure where the future instruction will lead. Teachers
are also concerned about the assignment of teachers. Although this
may be more an administrative problem than one for teacher education, we would point out that when a teacher does a poor job
because of insufficient training, it reflects on the entire profession.
It is not fair to the teacher or the pupil for a teacher to be assigned
to teach subjects which he is not prepared to teach.

*   *   *

WILLIAM J. WOODHAM, JR., SUPERINTENDENT OF SCHOOLS,
ESCAMBIA COUNTY, FLORIDA:

If I had my way, the conflict which has been going on between
institutional groups [the scholars and the professional educators] would
stop immediately. . . .

Classroom teachers, supervisors, administrators, and state department [of education] personnel would share with the faculties of
institutions of higher learning in planning programs for the preparation of teachers. . . .

Many opportunities would be provided for the college staff members in teacher education to have contact with the elementary and
secondary schools. . . .

Every student enrolled in the program of teacher education would
be taught by a superb teacher.

.   .   .

Procedures and instruments would be developed which would make
it possible to predict with a high degree of accuracy, at the time of
the completion of the pre-service teacher education program, the
probability of successful classroom performance. . . .

Salaries for teachers would be raised to a level comparable to that
of other professions so that the economic factor as a deterrent for a
student's selection of the teaching profession would be eliminated. . . .

The admission to membership in the professional organizations
would become an honored and sought-after privilege, rather than
an obligation as it now is in many instances. . . .

The recruitment and selection of prospective teachers would be a
continuous process, beginning in the elementary school and extending to the graduate-school level. . . .

* * *

SARAH C. CALDWELL, JUNIOR-HIGH-SCHOOL TEACHER,
AKRON, OHIO:

[For effective recruiting] . . . we must seek high-school students
with recognized academic ability. Certainly it is not too rigid to
require that they be within the upper 10 per cent of their class in
academic standing . . . [but] we must not allow ourselves to be so
blinded by evidence of academic ability that we consider it alone to
be sufficient. . . .

Personality traits must be stressed in the selection of teacher
education candidates. . . .

It must be our constant concern to draw into the profession persons
whose abilities and aptitudes point to the teaching profession. . . .

The first two years of the candidate's college experience [should]
be devoted chiefly to a general, broad education which would embrace
the humanities, the basic sciences, and the social studies. This would
be followed by specialization both in the candidate's own field of
interest and in professional education, if he is aiming at a teaching
career above the elementary level. Those wishing to teach in the
elementary school will require a thorough grounding in a variety
of subjects, in addition to the professional courses.

. . .

The courses [in professional education] must be constantly re-examined to make certain they are truly meaningful. We can no longer
close our eyes to a mere proliferation of courses which often fail to
serve the high-sounding purpose implied in their titles. . . .

[The] members [of the department of education faculty] must be
encouraged to apply self-criticism so that they may become aware of
the extent to which they may be violating in practice what they are
trying to teach in theory. For some of them, this may mean a return
visit to the classroom from which they may have been divorced far
too long. . . .

* * *

G. BALEY PRICE, CHAIRMAN, DEPARTMENT OF MATHEMATICS,
COLLEGE OF LIBERAL ARTS AND SCIENCES,
THE UNIVERSITY OF KANSAS:

[The elementary-school] teacher is usually not a specialist, and
almost all elementary-school teachers teach arithmetic. Many of these

teachers do not take any courses in arithmetic or mathematics in college, and, as a result, they are very poorly prepared to teach arithmetic. Under these circumstances it is understandable that they fear and dislike arithmetic. In many cases they do not teach much arithmetic to their pupils, but they do impart their fear and dislike of the subject. The result is serious because many students are turned against the study of mathematics permanently. . . .

Ways must be found to improve the competence of the elementary-school teacher to teach arithmetic.

Finally, if I had *my* way, I would improve the caliber of the students who enter teacher education and become teachers.

.   .   .

The first step in attracting more high-quality students to teacher education . . . is to make teacher education inherently more interesting and worthwhile. In order to do so, we must provide interesting and stimulating instructors to teach the courses. It is well known that many students do not like the education courses they are required to take for teacher education. Schools of education sometimes complain that departments of mathematics send them their weakest students and advise their best ones to seek industrial positions. It is unfortunately true that schools of education receive many of the weaker students, but not because they are sent by the departments of mathematics. Many good students are repelled by the education courses they are required to take. . . . And while the schools of education are improving their courses, the subject-matter departments must improve their courses and provide the best possible instructors to teach them.

*   *   *

HARRY N. RIVLIN, DEAN, DIVISION OF TEACHER EDUCATION, BOARD OF HIGHER EDUCATION, THE COLLEGES OF THE CITY OF NEW YORK:

If I had my way, the first change I should introduce is to eliminate all thought of what is feasible and what is practical as we begin to think of what we should do. If we begin by thinking of what we can do, we often wind up by thinking only of what we are doing. Instead of beginning our curriculum building, for example, by thinking of what administrative officers will accept, we should start by thinking of what needs to be done.

We should change the way in which we define the requirements for certification. In all too many instances, eligibility for a certificate is based upon the completion of so many credits in this subject and so many credits in that. As a result, we have people preparing to meet the letter of the law instead of preparing to become competent teachers. . . . Our present requirements assume, moreover, that the only way in which one learns is by taking courses, and [they] ignore the learning that comes from experience or from reading and independent study. No matter how much one may know of the philosophy and practices of modern education, it does not become official until a course has been taken, and it does not matter how long ago it was taken or what it included.

    .   .   .

For those candidates for certification who have not completed an appropriate program in an approved institution, the present requirements should be modified in two respects. First, no course should be acceptable if taken more than five years ago, unless the candidate has been teaching. Second, the requirement shoud be considered as having been met if the candidate passes a competence test in the field. A prospective teacher who has mastered a field should not be required to take even a single course he does not need.

    .   .   .

We should not underestimate our students or overestimate ourselves. We are so much concerned with what our students should know that we sometimes do not realize how much they already know.

    .   .   .

If I had *my* way, I should restrict admission to teacher education programs to those students who have the intellectual ability, scholarly background, and the personal qualities needed for effective teaching, and I should restrict appointments as teachers to those who are qualified and interested. . . . We have no way of knowing how many capable people are being dissuaded from going into teaching by the very attempts at increasing the size of the teaching force by lowering the standards for admission. Why should any superior student aspire to a position almost anybody can achieve? . . .

    *   *   *

WERNER A. BAUM, DEAN, GRADUATE SCHOOL AND DIRECTOR
OF RESEARCH, FLORIDA STATE UNIVERSITY (who restricted his
comments to the education of secondary-school teachers):

First, I would abolish the bachelor's degree in education for secondary-school teachers. The prospective teacher should be educated,
not trained. . . . Such education must include at least two ingredients: a sound general education, giving the prospective teacher a
broad view of man's cultural, social, and scientific heritage resulting
from thousands of years of struggle, and intensive study in at least
one of the intellectual disciplines. . . .

To reduce the question of teacher education to the popular
numbers game with credit hours . . . I am proposing that the student
devote approximately 40 semester hours to general education and
approximately 30 to one of the basic fields of knowledge. To this,
then, I would add approximately 20 hours of education, concentrated
in methods of teaching the subject field, educational psychology, and
supervised teaching, as a minor specifically oriented toward the
student's job aspirations. This makes a total of some 90 hours, leaving
considerable room for electives taken for sheer intellectual enjoy-
ment or for moderately intensive study of a second, related basic
field. . . .

My second action would be in the realm of administration, but
it is an absolutely necessary adjunct to the proposed standard of
teacher education. I would demechanize the salary scales for school
teachers. This change is necessary for the very practical reason that if
a competent young man has his degree in mathematics, rather than
mathematics education, we will not attract him to teaching for the
same salary we may pay a beginning English teacher. Whether this
is as it should be is entirely beside the point. Personally, I think
that philosophers are as important to mankind as physicists. But
society does not share that viewpoint. The inescapable fact is that
we live in a culture where money talks, much too loudly, and philosophers are generally paid less than physicists who, in turn, are
generally paid less than men in gray flannel suits. . . . We will not
attract educated mathematicians, physicists, and the like into the
secondary schools in numbers until we face the facts of the market
place.

.   .   .

Thirdly, I would require every teacher to have at least a year of
practical experience before admission to the graduate school. . . .

Fourth, I would expect the master's degree to be in education,
approximately half the work being in the basic discipline of specialization, the other half being in professional education. . . .

Fifth, I would have the graduate schools tigl.en both their admissions requirements and the quality of their degrees. I would restore dignity and significance to the master's degree by conferring it only upon that modest fraction of teachers of signal competence. . . . Recipients of the degree have the right to feel like one who has been listed in *Who's Who,* not like one who has been listed in the telephone directory.

Sixth, I would abolish school administration as a major field of study. . . . Competent school administrators can and should come up the instructional ladder. Graduate school is not the place for them to learn how to supervise janitors or fill out forms for the state department of education. The availability of this major, on the other hand, seduces teachers away from curricula they should be following to improve their teaching competence. . . .

Seventh and last, I would have the counties and states establish full-year graduate fellowships for promising teachers. The economics of our day makes it very difficult for most teachers to spend a full year in residence while pursuing graduate studies. The result is a conglomeration of extension credit, courses taken on a commuting basis, and attendance at double-speed summer sessions. It would be hard to conceive of a pattern less conducive to sound graduate study. . . .

* * *

DONALD P. COTTRELL, DEAN, COLLEGE OF EDUCATION, THE OHIO STATE UNIVERSITY:

. . . I think that we approach the education of the teacher on too low and too trivial a level. This goes for all of the content of the curriculum pursued by the prospective teacher. We belie our pretended interest in providing a good education for the teacher by obviously undervaluing and downgrading the role of the teacher ourselves. We know far more about good teaching than we teach and still more than we demonstrate. Some of us are so full of duplicity in our work that we tell our students outrightly that none of us, their teachers, knows anything substantial about how to teach—that is, the job we ourselves are engaged to do. If this is so, such people are quacks and have a moral responsibility to change occupations. But it is not so. People can and do learn how to be good teachers, when they obviously were not "born" to it, in the same fashion as they learn to do other things. It is time for all of us to "come clean" with our students who aspire to be teachers and join forthrightly with them in learning how to teach as well as possible.

*   *   *

JOHN H. FISCHER, SUPERINTENDENT OF PUBLIC INSTRUCTION, BALTIMORE, MARYLAND (Dr. Fischer became dean of Teachers College, Columbia University, on September 1, 1959):

. . . I shall not prescribe for all the ills of teacher education. Instead . . . I shall deal with the contributions teacher education might make toward improving elementary and secondary education in the large, cosmopolitan, urban school system. . . . In the first place, it is in the big city that American democracy now faces many of its toughest trials. . . . In the second place, the big city confronts the teacher with educational problems that require not only a superior combination of skills but a different approach to the teaching task itself. The metropolitan teacher cannot assume that this typical pupil will be the well-scrubbed, well-behaved, ambitious youngster the teacher probably was in his school-boy period. The greater chance is that many of his pupils will be culturally handicapped, poorly motivated, and, in all likelihood, below average in measurable intelligence. To be sure, there are bright, eager children in the cities. There are thousands of them, but they can be found and educated only by teachers who are willing and able to work in the social setting from which the slow and the reluctant as well as the quick and the ready students come to school.

The graduates of teacher education, in its traditional forms and in some of the newest patterns, are rarely prepared to cope with urban school problems. Indeed, they often view these tasks with distaste and reject as unworthy of their efforts the very children who most need to learn the value of learning. The attitude of many new teachers might be likened to that of a psychiatrist who would object to associating with mentally ill patients or a social worker who insisted on a case load of families with no domestic difficulties.

.   .   .

What education would I want, then, to prepare teachers for the responsibility of universal education in the American metropolis? I should begin, if I had my way, well upstream—with their elementary and secondary schooling. The best basic preparation for teaching does not differ from that which all citizens need to participate responsibly and well in social and political affairs. . . . The lower schools should encourage not only intellectual curiosity and interests but intellectual industry as well. These children especially should form the habit of striving for excellence as the only defensible goal.

When these people reach college, I would want for them the soundest possible liberal education so that having systematically examined man's past efforts to gain truth, understanding, and freedom they will themselves be more appreciative of truth and more conscientious about freedom. . . . And to avoid his becoming merely a jack-of-all-trades, I would want the prospective teacher to specialize in one field, at least to the extent of a respectable undergraduate major.

But a teacher—especially the one with whom I am particularly concerned—must be more than a well-educated person, more than a well-informed man or woman. The teacher has a specialized function to perform which is the unique obligation of his own profession. He can expect to be successful in it only as he masters the knowledge, procedures, and techniques essential to the practice of the profession. The enthusiastic dedication of the well-intentioned amateur is no more acceptable or effective in teaching than in engineering, surgery, or the law.

. . .

The teacher must also acquire those [disciplines] which enable him to understand growth and change in human beings, the dynamics of their behavior, the ways they learn, how they can be motivated, how their strengths can be nurtured and their weaknesses minimized. . . .

So, upon a firm liberal foundation I would have the teacher build strong professional competence, reserving most of the professional work for the graduate level. Beyond his generalized and specialized formal education, the prospective teacher will require practical experience with young people in varied situations. I would have this experience begin as early as high school, increasing in responsibility and culminating in a sustained period of student teaching or internship which would gradually shade into a full-fledged teaching assignment.

To extend the period of pre-service teacher education from the present four-year length to the five- or six-year program I prefer will be expensive, but not nearly as costly as the effects of incompetent teaching. My ready answer to the cost question [is] to propose a system of scholarships supported by federal funds. Briefly, I would permit any college student interested in a career in teaching at any level in any nonprofit institution to apply for a federal grant to cover at least full tuition in the college of his choice. Awards would be made to all . . . who meet specified minimum requirements. The allowance would become an interest-free, ten-year loan for those

who fail to enter or remain in teaching and an outright grant to
every successful student who teaches at least five years.

•   •   •

I do not propose that every person now being graduated and labeled
a teacher will need this rigorous training or one of these grants.
Many of the people who now accept classroom assignments are not
candidates for full professional status. A substantial fraction of the
people on school payrolls have no intention of enlisting for life, but
expect to serve the schools for a few years at most and then retire to
domestic or other duties for an indefinite period. Since this condition
is likely to persist, I suggest that we face it frankly and organize our
schools accordingly. The fully prepared and committed teachers
I would assign as senior or leading teachers, to work with groups of
the other staff members whose qualifications are of a lower order
and whose responsibilities would be limited in proportion.

•   •   •

Every teacher, especially the senior teachers I describe, will need
continuous access to further formal education and other forms of
personal growth. Such advanced work should include graduate study,
research, travel, and participation in local, state, national, and international affairs. The expense of this program should be shared and
budgeted at every governmental level and administered to assure every
career teacher periodic opportunities for further development.

•   •   •

I would involve the teacher, as a part of his advanced on-the-job
development, in a variety of social and civic enterprises. The purposes
of this work would be to enable the teacher to better know the total
metropolitan complex and those who live in it, to see the special
role of the school, and to appreciate the work of other agencies
which join with the school in meeting the needs of young people.
But all this would be done in time provided for the purpose and not
as an overtime assignment. . . .

And, if I had my way, I would not hesitate to use the public purse
to subsidize the education of teachers, for I favor economy in the
expenditure of tax funds. I can conceive of no use to which the same
amount of money could be put that would produce remotely comparable results in private profit or public benefit.

CHAPTER SEVEN

The Three R's—and Then Some

There has been considerable talk in recent years about "the good ol' three R's," especially to the effect that a "return" to them would be the cure for all of our educational ills. There are those, of course, who insist that we have never been away from them, so how can we return? This difference of viewpoint makes for spirited discussion and sometimes has resulted in the bitter exchange of words in national magazines. Regardless of this debate, from the way some folks toss off the expression, "the three R's," you might get the idea that readin', 'ritin', and 'rithmetic are simple and uncomplicated, and, like Grandma's biscuits, they must be good because they are old-fashioned. Old-fashioned they are not, and simple and uncomplicated they also are not.

Nothing is so basic, so vital, in the education of American youth as English. This is more than just 'readin' and 'ritin'; it is a love of reading, the ability to communicate and to understand, and an appreciation of literature. Knowledge of the language is the foundation on which all other education must stand.

To brush off the vast and complex field of mathematics as 'rithmetic is to ignore the sweeping changes that research has brought in the past quarter-century. Algebra and geometry have dropped down from the upper grades of high school and are being introduced in elementary school and junior high. Calculus is dropping from college to high school—and how many of today's parents have even *heard* of a course called "Probability and Statistical Analysis," which some of their teen-agers are studying?

The "three R's" that Grandpa studied are not good enough for today's youth. (They were not good enough for Grandpa either, when you get right down to it.) And, with all due respect to our elders, it is recognized that the teacher of yesteryear would be lost in today's classroom, particularly in those schools which have honor courses and college-level programs for the gifted students able to forge ahead. Franklin D. Murphy summed it up when he told the Kansas Conference: "From earliest times, man, of course, has been engaged in mining new knowledge, but it is as though in these later years he has suddenly struck a vein of unprecedented length and breadth."

Today's high-school teachers must be better prepared than ever before in the fields they are teaching; they need to dig deeply into their subjects, to know much more than they will ever be called upon to use in the classroom. The problem of preparing such a teacher was the primary concern of the Kansas Conference, just as it was at Bowling Green the year before. Before the meeting got under way, each participant was given a set of working papers, which outlined what various institutions across the country were doing in the field of subject-matter specialization. Let us consider some of those programs, and see what the high-school teacher of the "three R's" needs to know to do his job.

First, the program for prospective high-school English teachers at Fenn College, Cleveland, Ohio:

Fenn College believes that every teacher of English in secondary schools should have a major in English, and every American child should have the right to be taught by a professional teacher of English. The subject is invaluable as an end in itself, but it also is basic to all other learning. If English is poorly taught, the pupil will be handicapped in his other subjects.

What, then, is an English teacher?

Fenn College believes that he is a well-read person, a reader of insight and comprehension. He must be acquainted with the literature of our language, its history, its forms, its ideas. He has developed critical principles, with the ability to distinguish the excellent from the gaudy and the false. He must love to read, and he must be able to develop this love in his students, whether they be the brilliant and able or the slow and dull. He must be able to teach his students the nature of their own language, not merely for the sake of correctness but to enable them to use its full resources with confidence. He must be able to write and speak exceptionally well.

To major in English at Fenn College, the prospective teacher must have 60 quarter hours (40 semester hours) of courses which include:

Course	Quarter Hours
English composition	9
English literature	6
American literature	6
Modern American novel	3
Advanced composition	3
History of the English language	3
Wordsworth and Coleridge	3
Byron, Shelley, and Keats	3

Course	Quarter Hours
Shakespeare	6
English literature before 1830	6
Electives	12

The minor requires 42 quarter hours (28 semester hours), which is the same as the above through Shakespeare. No grade below a "C" is counted as fulfilling a course requirement in either a major or a minor.

The program of general education at Fenn College strengthens and broadens this specialization. It includes a working knowledge of French, German, or Spanish; public speaking; fine arts; philosophy or religion; natural science; American government; U. S. history; economics; psychology; sociology; and European history. The professional education program consists of 26 quarter hours (17 semester hours) and includes purposes and practices of education, educational psychology, measurements and evaluation, special methods of teaching, and student teaching.

Professor Donald Tuttle of Fenn College pointed out that, although an English teacher should have a major in the subject, this is not always possible. Because of the number of small high schools, because teaching loads do not always come out evenly, and because there is sometimes a shortage of qualified English teachers, some teachers with only a minor in the course are assigned to teach English. For these reasons, the minor programs must be worked out very carefully, and so planned that the teacher can take graduate work in the subject. Some English teachers, Tuttle said, get into the field by accident. They have accumulated a motley collection of courses that add up to the right number of hours, and some colleges will recommend them for a teaching certificate in English even if those courses form no defensible pattern and even if their grades are low in the subject. If the minor program does not permit graduate work, the teacher may limp along unprepared in his subject throughout his career.

With the programs it has devised, an excellent faculty, and a hand-picked student body, it is obvious that Fenn College is graduating the type of English teacher that this country so desperately needs. But it is a tragic commentary on our times and values that these graduates are being lured into other fields by higher pay and brighter futures. As Tuttle pointed out:

Some . . . take positions in advertising, public relations, journalism, radio and television, and—especially if they have studied some accounting and economics—in business or industry. As I write, there is a request on my desk from a greeting card company for ten English majors. Our most promising English major this year will probably work for the Cleveland *Press;* one of the finest in recent years went to work for a trade journal, of which Cleveland has many.

The working papers included a description of the program at the University of Illinois for preparing future high-school mathematics teachers.

The theory of the teacher at Illinois is that:

Without minimizing the importance of his duties in the classroom, his duties as the guide and adviser of the *most promising* mathematics students is held to be of the highest importance. To be a trustworthy guide, the teacher must have an acquaintance with mathematics for a considerable distance beyond the point he is likely to reach in the classroom.

At first glance this emphasis on the most promising student seems a bit undemocratic, and perhaps it is. Certainly the gifted student in any field of study must be pushed and prodded to his utmost effort, but it should not be at the *expense* of the other students. (In a somewhat similar vein, a scientist at the Kansas Conference said the job of an English teacher "is to acquaint individuals with good literature; to teach them to write articles which are clear, concise, and short; to inculcate the ability to communicate with the spoken and written word." His audience disagreed, in the conviction that such teaching would produce efficient and articulate research assistants but not well-rounded persons. Does the Illinois theory operate to produce more mathematicians, or well-rounded individuals?)

The Illinois mathematics curriculum is a five-year program. It includes, in the first four years, 20 hours of professional education and 35 hours of mathematics (this is a bit less than most mathematicians want in the major). The fifth year requires eight units of graduate work: two in education, four in mathematics, and two unrestricted electives. For a minor in mathematics, 18 semester hours are required, but 21 are recommended. This is also a little less than most mathematicians feel is enough.

Among the mathematics requirements are eight semester hours of calculus, six hours of fundamental concepts (devoted to supplying background for the teacher), and six hours each of advanced algebra and advanced Euclidian geometry. The graduate program includes two semester hours either of introduction to higher algebra or of introduction to higher geometry, a two-hour mathematics elective, and a two-hour unrestricted elective, which might be in mathematics. Most fifth-year students take *both* higher algebra and higher geometry. The introduction to higher algebra, incidentally, deals with "groups, rings, fields, linear transformation," and introduction to higher geometry is "projective geometry, analytic and synthetic."

And all this, just to teach something called "the third R"!

. . . AND THEN SOME MORE—

Science: In a period so brief it is but a twinkle in the eye of history, science has re-shaped life on earth and reached out for the distant stars. If Rip Van Winkle had started his famous twenty-year snooze in 1940, he would have awakened to a new world which took for granted such things as radar, jet flight, earth satellites, frozen foods, atomic fission, hydrogen bombs, automation, polio vaccine, and television.

How can a high-school science teacher explain these modern miracles to his students? What does he need to know? It is not enough to present material and ask questions; he must stimulate and guide his students, knowing full well all the while the severe limitations of his own knowledge. As an example:

To earn a Bachelor of Science degree in science teaching at the University of Arizona, the future teacher must have 125 units for graduation, of which 52 must be in science, 21 in professional education, and the balance in general education. These are the science courses he must take in the four-year program: freshman year— introduction to mathematics and foundations of physical science; sophomore year—introduction to biological science or mathematical analysis, principles of chemistry or physics; junior year—principles of physics (or chemistry or genetics), chemistry or biology elective, and another science elective; senior year—development of science and science electives.

To qualify for a permanent secondary-school certificate in Arizona, the student must complete 30 hours of graduate work. This leads the student deeply into the fields of biology, chemistry, mathematics, or physics.

Such is the headlong race that science is making toward new frontiers; it must be considered impossible that a science teacher could ever complete his education.

Foreign Languages: Some say that knowing a foreign language is a question of national survival, and it must be acknowledged that it is difficult to sell someone on the merits of democracy by using sign language. That is just about what was happening in the

Middle East a few years ago during one of those periodic flare-ups which may someday turn into a war. The United States had just one man in that vast area who spoke Arabic; the Russians had more than 100. It is also a question of convenience. I know a man who thought he was ordering dessert in a Paris cafe and the waiter brought him two fried eggs. Whatever the reason, there is no doubt that foreign languages are crowding themselves into the school programs—there are more students studying a second language in elementary schools than there are in college, and more in high school than in the grades.

At Purdue University, where marvellous things are being done in the teaching of foreign languages, there is heavy emphasis on conversation and composition. The program is deliberately tough, and it has attracted the most able students. The State Board of Education sets a minimum of 36 semester hours for a major in a foreign language, and Purdue does not feel this is enough for any teacher outside the genius class: "The reason is obvious when we reflect that college students are frequently deficient in the use of *English,* which they have spoken since the age of two and studied since the age of six." A course has been added to the Purdue curriculum in which the teacher candidates rehearse and perform simple playlets in Spanish, eventually taking their show on the road to neighboring high schools. This gives the student a practical tool to use in his later teaching, and it requires linguistic ability of a high order. The Purdue course rests on the premise that quality and demonstrated proficiency are the goals, not a set number of courses and hours.

Social Studies: Science has done so much to make life comfortable for us that there often seems to be a temptation to turn the world over to the scientists and let them run it. But, as one of the speakers at the Kansas Conference (Corey) pointed out:

Science is helpless, or virtually so, in the realm of the aesthetic, the moral, and the abstract. We cannot expect science to raise the moral or aesthetic level of a people or of the world. The present confused state of human affairs is straining the faith which intellectuals of an earlier day had in the efficacy of science to solve all human ills.

Man lives in the present with his roots anchored deeply in the past; if it is true that "the past is prologue," it also is true that man's heritage is not made to measure and presented to him at birth, but handed down generation by generation over the centuries. And what must a teacher know in order to interpret the present in the light of what has gone before? The conferees at the Kansas Conference were fairly well agreed that a teacher of the social studies should have a broad background in history, economics, geography, political science, sociology, geography, and anthropology. Several discussion groups proposed 60 semester hours of specialization in one area for a major, and one proposed that the minor be at least 48 semester hours.

This is considerably stronger than the program at the University of Nebraska, which was presented to the participants in one of the working papers. This may be because Nebraska certification regulations require that each teacher candidate be prepared to teach in "two generally recognized high-school subject fields," with the advice that the student specialize in two unrelated fields. This regulation might tend to ease the teacher shortage, but it prevents a teacher candidate from becoming a real expert in his field.

There are really three types of programs for teacher candidates majoring in the social sciences at Nebraska. There is a broad major which requires 48 semester hours of work, including 15 of history; 6 each of economics, political science, and geography; 3 of sociology; and 12 hours in any two of these fields. This program is taken by about 80 per cent of the teacher candidates in social science. The second alternative is a single major in history, totaling 26 hours. Students are advised to take additional work in related fields, but are not required to do so. The third program is a 24-hour major in political science, economics, geography, or sociology, with a required minor in history and another minor in some other field. These programs appear to be a bit thin, and certainly they are considerably less than most of the Bowling Green conferees were willing to accept.

Two other subject-matter programs, in brief:

Physical Education: A high-school teacher of physical education must (or should) be a person of many talents. Like all teachers he must have a broad, liberal education, and he must have the professional background in education that makes him a skilled teacher. It is not enough that, on top of this, he knows the rules and regulations of basketball, football, baseball, archery, and the like. At the University of Oregon, for instance, he must take 3 quarter credits in algebra, 12 in general biology, 12 in elementary chemistry, 6 in human physiology, and 6 in human anatomy. In addition, he needs a strong background in nutrition, personal hygiene community hygiene, communicable diseases, first aid or care and prevention of injuries, school health services, and the health instruction program.

Business Education: A four-year program of preparation for a high-school teacher of business subjects? It cannot be done, because there is not time, reported Kansas State Teachers College in one of the conference working papers; the bachelor's degree is only a beginning point of professional preparation, growth, and development. Business education is more than just typing, shorthand, and bookkeeping—much more. A discussion group at the Kansas Conference said it should "further an understanding of the fundamental concepts, beliefs, and appreciations which are essential to the conduct of daily personal business affairs, to increase the understanding of citizenship in a democracy, and to develop vocational skills and knowledge in business. . . ." Kansas State Teachers College requires 50 semester hours of general education and 20 hours of professional education (which is just about what the Kansas conferees thought was proper). This leaves 50 hours for specialization which, in addition to mastery of the various business skills, must include an understanding in depth of the capitalist system, and the political, social, and economic privileges and responsibilities of the free-enterprise system. And let us have no rash talk about business education being a frill—the multitudes who work in the many fields of business make up the largest segment of the employed population of the United States.

The programs and suggestions outlined in this chapter represent some of the "what to teach" aspects of the preparation of high-school teachers, which must complement and strengthen the "how to teach" program. Except for a few die-hards on the outer fringes of reason and common sense, no one even remotely concerned with teacher education believes you can get by with one without the other. It is true that the arguments about "methods" versus "subject matter" have been raging for years, but it is a question of emphasis, not substitution or elimination.

Why, then, are so many teachers ill-prepared to teach their subjects? The blame usually is placed squarely at the door of teacher education institutions, particularly the single-purpose "teachers colleges." In some cases, no doubt, this is justified—and it is certainly an easy thing to do. But it is not the teachers college which grants a certificate to a former science teacher who left the profession 20 years ago and now wants to teach again on the basis of out-dated credits. It is not the teachers college which admits to the classroom a teacher who never finished a four-year college course. It is not the teachers college which tells an English teacher to take on classes in a foreign language just because he is the only one available who has had a college course in French, however brief and however many years ago. The one and only purpose of the conferences at Bowling

Green, Kansas, and San Diego was to produce a better teacher education program. The colleges and universities can produce better teachers; it is for the parents, the schools, and the school boards to insist that only the better teachers be hired.

CHAPTER EIGHT

It's Elementary, My Dear Teacher

A tourist once got lost in the hill country of West Virginia and stopped to ask a farmer how to get back to the main highway. The farmer cogitated for awhile, selecting possible routes and discarding them, and finally declared, "Mister, you can't get there from here." Many educators feel the same way about squeezing an "academic major" into the program of a college student preparing to teach in elementary school.

Granted the elementary-school teacher does not need good, solid study in depth in a particular field to the same degree that a high-school teacher does; granted she needs numerous courses in professional education to prepare her for the young and immature minds she must teach and develop; granted, too, that she needs a broad education in the many subjects she will teach. Even so, specialization *can* be acquired, and at the Kansas Conference there was considerable insistence that it should be. But even in the discussion groups which agreed on the need for specialization, there was disagreement on precisely what "specialization" is. Some took it to mean the specific preparation of the teacher to teach elementary-school children in the classroom. Others were talking about academic specialization in a particular field, and those who advocated this seemed reluctant to specify any particular number of semester hours that should be devoted to it. One group put it this way:

We believe we should work toward a major in an academic discipline for the elementary-school teacher. This recommendation is based upon our basic assumption that an elementary-school teacher should be a truly educated person, and our belief that scholarship in depth in some one discipline contributes to one's personal growth as such a vital and educated person. The criterion for such a major is both usability for teaching and the personal development of the teacher.

Other groups contented themselves with the general recommendation that the elementary-school teacher have depth in one or more areas.

Purdue University a few years ago began preparing elementary-school teachers and included a 24-semester-hour academic major in the program (which also includes 40 hours of professional education). The subject of the major is chosen by the student. In presenting the Purdue program to the conference, Elton Hocking, chairman of the Department of Modern Languages, told the conference:

This unusual provision results from the conviction of our faculty that not only does a major field add to the professional development of *any* teacher, but also that "teachers are people" and that the unique values of an academic major, enjoyed by all other undergraduates, should not be denied to any prospective teacher.

Of the academic subjects available as majors, two of the most popular choices are French and Spanish. This is fortunate, for in perhaps no field is the teacher shortage more acute than in the field of "FLES"—foreign languages in the elementary schools. Enrollments have skyrocketed in the last six or seven years . . . [and] needless to say, there are not nearly enough elementary-school teachers who are qualified to teach and speak a foreign language correctly, so that many—perhaps most—of the children are learning to mispronounce their foreign language and perhaps to hate it, too.

It is true, of course, that a foreign language teacher in an elementary school probably is primarily responsible for the instruction of her specialty and not so likely to be teaching all the subjects in the elementary-school curriculum. Because of the difficulty of her task, and her unique position on the staff, an academic major is perhaps more important to her than to any other teacher. But note, too, that Purdue offers majors in other fields; French and Spanish just happen to be the most popular.

A somewhat different type of specialization is that for teachers of the mentally retarded, as reported by the University of Missouri. All elementary-school teacher candidates at Missouri are required to take 44 semester hours of general education, broken down as follows:

Course	Semester Hours
Introduction to education	2
English	9
American history	5
American government	5
Mathematics	3
Science	10
Fine arts	5
Health education	2
Geography	3

Also required are 32 hours of professional education, plus 15 hours in a required minor in an academic field. For those who expect to qualify as teachers of mentally retarded children, there is an additional requirement of 31 hours, including such courses as psychology of exceptional children, speech correction, and student teaching with the retarded.

Stanford University has found a way to give elementary-school teacher candidates real depth in academic disciplines—make it a five-year program. This program will be dealt with in detail in a later chapter; let us note here only that it includes 51 semester hours of general education, required of all students; 35 hours of extended general education, required for elementary-school teachers and providing for additional work in the humanities and social sciences; *and* 20 hours in advanced courses in one area of knowledge to be selected in consultation with the faculty adviser. The Stanford program is also designed so that prospective teachers who wish to take their bachelor's degree in something other than elementary education have available such broadly conceived bachelor's degree programs as the humanities honors program, the social sciences-general program, or the physical sciences-general program.

Even where an academic major cannot be worked into the program, some schools have emphasized a degree in depth for elementary-school teachers. At Central Missouri State College, for instance, such teachers must take at least 21 hours of English and 13 hours of work in social science.

At Iowa State Teachers College the student who plans to teach in elementary schools major in elementary education; however, the program is so arranged that the student *can* do considerable studying in depth in an academic field—almost as much as a secondary-school teacher majoring in that subject. Each student is required to take a general education program consisting of 43 semester hours of work and including English, mathematics, science, social science, and electives in the humanities. In addition he is required to complete 15 semester hours in a subject-matter field (24 hours if the field is a foreign language). Also required is a series of courses called "Supplementary General Education," totaling 20 semester hours in geography, science, children's literature, foundations of arithmetic, art, foundations of music, and child psychology. By choosing carefully his courses in general education, supplementary general education, the 15-hour study in an academic field, and his free electives, the student can cover considerable ground in one area of concentration. By the same token, the student could dabble in any number of things and fall short of even a respectable minor. It would appear, however, that the program could be an excellent one, given the services of good guidance officers or student advisers. Iowa State Teachers College has added a "professional semester" of 17 hours also to be taken in the junior or senior year just before the student begins his student teaching. In this semester are lumped many of the methods courses that will be of particular value to him when he begins his laboratory experience.

There is a considerable body of opinion, of course, which holds that the elementary-school teacher does not need an academic major or study in depth in any particular field nearly so much as he needs a general education in many areas. And it must be conceded that a third-grade pupil will ask his teacher a million and one questions about everything under the sun without probing very deeply into anything.

It seems to be with this idea in mind that the National College of Education in Evanston, Illinois, has drawn up its program for elementary-school teachers. Taken from the Bowling Green working papers, here is the undergraduate curriculum of prescribed courses:

Freshman Year

First Semester: art in the elementary school, 2 hours; essentials of speech, 2; communication, 2; humanities, 3; human growth and development (with a significant amount of observation), 3; sociology, 3; physical education, 1; total, 16.

Second Semester: same as first semester.

Sophomore Year

First Semester: childhood education, 2 hours; music essentials, 2; humanities, 3; biological science, 3; American life and institutions, 3; play activities in the elementary school, 2; chorus, 1; total, 16.

Second Semester: childhood education—participation, 1 hour; literature for children, 3; social studies in the elementary school, 3; humanities, 3; biological science, 3; American life and institutions, 3; total, 16.

Junior Year

First Semester: arithmetic in the elementary school, 2 hours; language arts in the elementary school, 4; physical science, 2; general mathematics, 2; science elective, 3; free elevtives, 3; total, 16.

Second Semester: music in the elementary school, 2 hours, student teaching and conference, 3; physical science, 2; science elective, 3; free electives, 6; total, 16.

Senior Year

First Semester: all-day student teaching and conference—9 weeks, 7 hours; educational measurements, 3; science for teachers, 3; free electives, 3; total, 16.

Second Semester: professional seminar for seniors, 3 hours; social science elective, 3; literature elective, 3; free electives, 7; total, 16.

It does not appear that even a weak major in one of the academic subjects is available here, even if the 19 hours in free electives are concentrated in one area of study. In "Summary of Requirements in Teacher Education Curricula," published by The National Council for Accreditation of Teacher Education in 1958, the National College of Education is listed as requiring 37 hours of professional education and 92 hours in general education. However, the program outlined above would indicate that at least 18 of those 92 hours of "general education" are in such courses as "Art in the Elementary School," "Literature for Children," etc. This would seem to be stretching a point, or a definition.

The question of whether an academic major can be squeezed into the elementary-school teacher's program thus seems to depend on the philosophy of each individual institution.

CHAPTER NINE

Student Teaching—The Crux

If there was one point of unanimous agreement at the Kansas Conference, it was on the value of student teaching ("practice teaching"). But there was much less than unanimity on when and where it should be fitted into the future teacher's program.

With few exceptions, student teaching now comes in the student's last year of a four-year course. Suppose he finds, at this late date, that he cannot abide the little monsters? Is he likely to face the facts, switch to some other field, and start all over again? Or will he decide that since he has gone this far he might as well stick with it, at least until something better turns up? And if he does stick with it, how do you calculate the harm to the thousands of children who will pass through his classroom? This is an extreme example—most such students would not elect to become teachers in the first place, or they would be weeded out before they got into their senior year. But it represents a risk, however slight, that should never be taken.

It is obviously impossible to drop student teaching down to the freshman or sophomore year, when the student would know neither what to teach nor how to teach it. Neither is he likely to be well enough prepared during his junior year. The solution would seem to be to "expose" prospective teachers to the classroom early in their college careers to see whether, like the measles, it will "take." This was recommended by several discussion groups, and many such programs are, in fact, now in operation.

At Pacific Lutheran College, in Parkland, Washington, for instance, every teacher candidate gets the following "laboratory experience":

1. As a part of the "Introduction to Education" course, he spends a minimum of two hours a week working with a group of children in a community agency or school.
2. When he takes "Human Growth and Development" he again returns to the classroom, studies children, and observes their growth patterns from kindergarten through junior-high-school. He spends at least two hours a week on the junior-high-school level, and "as much time as necessary" with the smallest fry.

3. When he takes "Methods and Observation," he once more spends at least two hours a week in classroom observation. This time he observes teaching as well as children.

4. Before the opening of the college year in which he is to take his student teaching, the student must spend a minimum of two weeks in a public school, getting firsthand knowledge of the problems and organization of a classroom at the beginning of a school year.

5. As a part of "Curriculum, Methods and Student Teaching" he spends the afternoons of sixteen weeks observing and teaching one group of children on his *less preferred* level of teaching. He also observes teaching in other grades and subject-matter fields.

6. As a student teacher, he observes and teaches forenoons on his *preferred* level for sixteen weeks, and for two weeks spends the entire day in school.

The certificate granted after this course of study legally allows the graduate to teach at all levels, kindergarten through high school, hence the student teaching experience on *preferred* and *less preferred* levels. The faculty at Pacific Lutheran College also believes that experience on the two levels gives the student a broader and deeper appreciation of the whole school and the work of teachers at different levels.

Marshall College in Huntington, West Virginia, has a somewhat similar program. At Marshall, students enrolled in the first course in "Human Development" associate with children and youth in playgrounds, in kindergartens, in privately operated nursery schools, and in such organizations as Boy and Girl Scout troops, 4H Clubs, YMCA, and YWCA. In their junior year at college, teacher candidates participate in "junior student teaching," which involves from 35 to 40 hours of classroom activity where the students direct the learning activities of a group of children for at least 10 to 15 clock hours. Marshall College also has a "September experience" for prospective teachers, in which they spend the opening week at a public school near their home. This comes between their second and third year at college, or between their third and fourth year.

Programs such as these certainly answer some worrisome questions, but they raise another just as worrisome: Does not all this take too much time out of a student's four-year program?

Dean Clapp of Grinnell College, telling what he would do "If I had my way," acknowledged the great importance of student teaching, but added he was "rather less convinced that it is a responsibility of the college within the four-year framework":

[After all,] we do not feel called on to provide practice at a teller's window for our students who want to be bankers, or a starvation diet in a dormitory garret for those who want to write. So I would probably join the movement to foster on-the-job apprenticeships for those fine teachers we have been talking about.

Dean Clapp undoubtedly has a good point. Still, it is debatable whether he would take his toothache to a dentist who was getting his practical experience on the job, or submit to the healing art of a young doctor who had read all about appendectomies, but had never seen one performed. Teachers, of course, are not doctors or dentists; neither are they bankers or writers.

There seemed to be no effort made at the Kansas Conference to specify a set number of hours, weeks, or days that a student teacher should spend in the laboratory classroom. Several speakers said the experience should last at least six weeks, and should come as close as possible to real teaching—making lesson plans, grading papers, and other fundamentals of the job. But the length of time depends entirely on what goes into the student teaching. At George Peabody College for Teachers, student teaching has been expanded to a full three months by consolidating several individual courses into the program. Several conference participants gave this their full approval. Such methods courses as "How to Teach English" and "How to Teach Arithmetic," they said, can be abolished if the teacher candidate is taught how to teach these subjects in an actual classroom, under the supervision of an *excellent* professional classroom teacher.

That *excellent* teacher is an essential ingredient in any student teaching program. It is not enough that the student see and hear good classroom techniques; he must himself be taught. Some schools of education have found it pays to offer cooperating teachers tuition-free workshops and special courses dealing with student teaching. Most states do not pay the cooperating teachers, but again, many individual institutions have found it to be a good practice. This seems only reasonable; the teacher not only teaches the student, he also acts (or should act) as a counselor and adviser.

G. Baley Price, chairman of the Mathematics Department at the University of Kansas, told the conference of his concern with student teaching in its present form:

Although practice teaching usually occupies not more than half a semester, it interferes seriously with the teaching of mathematics at any time during the senior year. Mathematics has a strong sequential character, and it is necessary, for maximum understanding, that courses be taken in a prescribed order. But some students do their practice teaching during the first semester and others during the second semester. As a result of the interruptions from practice teaching and the necessity to teach mathematics in a specified order, not even the large departments of mathematics can provide the courses required to educate properly the future secondary-school mathematics teacher. The future seems to demand that four years, uninterrupted by practice teaching, be available for these courses.

Price was speaking only for mathematics, but it is probable that the same point could be made for other areas of study, particularly in the sciences.

There is great variety in the student-teaching practices of the 1,147 teacher education institutions across the country, as reflected in a survey by the National Council for Accreditation of Teacher Education (NCATE) for the 1957-58 academic year. The survey included 294 of the institutions accredited by the council. It showed that the predominant practice among the 294 institutions is to conduct their student-teaching programs in off-campus schools. The next largest group used a combination of campus and off-campus schools and the least-used procedure was to use campus schools exclusively.

The length of the student teaching experience ranged from a low of one to four weeks to a high of 45 to 49 weeks, but there was only a scattering of schools at these extremes—the heaviest cluster was in the 15 to 19 week range. The predominant practice seemed to be to require five days a week of student teaching, ranging between three and six hours a day.

An experimental program in student teaching, worked out by the municipal colleges and the public schools of New York City, seems to hold great promise for many big cities which have hard-to-staff "problem schools." Basically it is very simple: college seniors do their student teaching at the same schools to which they will be assigned after they have secured their licenses.

Dr. Harry N. Rivlin, dean of teacher education for the colleges, has said:

The present experiment rests on a very simple assumption. When there is a shortage of teachers, and young teachers can choose the schools in which they will teach, they stay away from the schools they think of as being difficult. In most cases, they are exhibiting fear of the unknown rather than sound professional judgment. What we are doing is to make student teaching in these schools a worthwhile professional experience. We are giving our students the professional help they need in order to succeed in these schools and to see the satisfactions that come to the teachers there. Finally, with the co-operation of the board of education, we can assure them that they will be appointed to the specific school they have come to know instead of facing assignment anywhere.

The experiment got under way in the spring of 1960 when five seniors from Hunter College were assigned to do their student teaching at James Fenimore Cooper Junior High School. Four of the five began teaching there full time in the fall, with the fifth to follow when she completed her studies at Hunter College in February, 1961. Cooper Junior High was especially chosen as typical of a big-city school where there is a high turnover of teachers.

"If the project succeeds," Dr. Rivlin said, "we have a technique that has implications, not only for this city, but for Detroit, Chicago, Philadelphia, and all the other big cities which are facing the same problem. Virtually every city has difficulty in recruiting teachers for those areas where social and economic conditions mean that children need unusually sympathetic, understanding, and competent teachers."

The project would appear to make great good sense: a beginning teacher thoroughly familiar with the particular kinds of problems he must face is going to be that much better a teacher.

CHAPTER TEN

It Takes Four—and More

A broad and liberal general education . . . a study in depth in at least one academic field . . . competence in a foreign language . . . solid preparation in professional education . . . classroom experiences with children, climaxed by a lengthy period of student teaching . . . all these things, and more, go into the preparation of the kind of teacher demanded for today's schools. A five-year period of preparation, accepted as a good idea at Bowling Green, became an essential when delegates to the Kansas Conference tried to piece together an ideal program of teacher education.

"If we need more time, we must take more time," said one participant. "It is worse than ridiculous to emasculate one important element of teacher education in order to strengthen another." Said another: "To extend the program to five or six years would be expensive, but not as costly as the effects of incompetent teaching." And another, in presenting a possible program: "Time will surely run out in four years."

The discussion groups found themselves in agreement. A five-year program, they said, is "essential," "inevitable," "rapidly becoming a necessity." But here again, as was so often the case at Kansas, the discussion groups were not agreed on just what the fifth year should be. Some wanted it to follow a year of actual teaching. The teacher would be aware of his strengths and weaknesses, they said, and better able to fit a program to his needs. Others wanted five straight years of preparation before the teacher embarked on his career, but there was disagreement here, too. Some wanted a four-year liberal arts progam with an academic major, followed by a year of professional education, including student teaching. Others wanted an integrated program, combining a general education, an area of specialization, and professional education for the entire five years. Discussions oft-times bogged down, too, on the question of graduate programs. As it now stands, a teacher who wants a higher degree—and the increased salary that goes with it—must take his work in a graduate department, even though what he wants and really needs is an undergraduate course he did not have time for before.

The necessity of a fifth year, and the problems of working it out, have been discussed in a previous chapter. Let us consider here some five-year programs that have attracted considerable praise and attention—first, the program for an elementary-school certificate at Stanford University, Palo Alto, California.

As reported in a conference working paper, the Stanford faculty decided—as have many others—that it is neither possible nor desirable to prepare elementary-school teachers in four years. In 1952 Stanford set up a five-year program which is still in effect and which, from the start, has had the endorsement of the California State Department of Education, which was happy to see a private institution ready and willing to take on such a pioneering project. The program includes one year of graduate study and leads to two degrees, the B.A. in education and the M.A. in education. Requirements for the B.A. are in four parts, as shown in this illustrative program:

General Studies Program (University Requirements): social science, 8 semester hours (history of Western civilization); humanities, 25 (English, foreign language, electives); natural sciences, 12 (biology, physical sciences); foreign language, mathematics, or logic, 3; senior colloquia, 3; total, 51 semester hours. Four non-credit activity hours also are required.

Extended General Education: social sciences, 16 semester hours (political science or history, anthropology or sociology, psychology, child psychology, and geography); mathematics, 3; physical education, 3 (modern dance, folk dance, rhythms, and sports skills); humanities, 13 (linguistics, philosophy, poetry, literature, art, music); total, 35 semester hours.

Additional Concentrated Study: Advanced courses in one area of knowledge to be selected in consultation with the adviser, 20 semester hours.

Professional Education: elementary school in America, development in middle childhood, social foundations of education, health foundations of education, philosophy of education, and psychological foundations of education; total of 15 semester hours.

The grand total of the requirements in the four areas above is 121 semester hours. The requirements of the master's degree in elementary education total 32 semester hours, as in the following illustration:

Fall Quarter: participation in the elementary school, 4 semester hours (two five-week, half-day assignments as a teacher's assistant, one in the primary grades and the other in an intermediate grade); curriculum and instruction in elementary schools, $5\frac{1}{3}$ (reading, related language arts, arithmetic); audio-visual laboratory, $\frac{2}{3}$.

Winter Quarter: Curriculum and instruction in elementary schools, $5\frac{1}{3}$ (social studies and science); music in the elementary school, 2; art in the elementary school, 2; physical education in the elementary school, 2.

Spring Quarter: Directed teaching, 10⅔ (full-time assignment for three months as a student teacher).

This program answers many of the critics of teacher education for elementary-school teachers: the four-year undergraduate program requires only 15 hours of professional education (with no break for student teaching); it provides a broad, general education; and it allows a study in depth of an academic subject. The fifth-year program includes preliminary work in the classroom, and a sustained period of student teaching. Most of the prospective elementary-school teachers enrolled at Stanford prefer to take their B.A. in education, but provision has been made for those who prefer to major in some other department. Such students are encouraged to take the 15 semester hours of professional education as electives while taking their degrees in the humanities honors program, the social sciences-general program, or the physical sciences-general program.

The School of Education at Stanford has not tried to develop special subject-matter courses for prospective teachers; it prefers that they take these courses with future lawyers, doctors, social workers, and the like.

A few years after the five-year plan was put into effect, it was modified to some extent for those able or gifted students who were ready for a more complete involvement with classroom work than the regular program permitted. These students return to the campus for a special summer session immediately after graduation with a B.A. degree, serve as "intern" teachers during the next regular school year in the Palo Alto Unified School District, and return for another summer session of study leading to the M.A. As interns they have full responsibility for a classroom program, and are paid by the school district at 75 per cent of the regular salary for beginning teachers. For every four such interns hired, a master teacher in the district is released from teaching duties and works with the university supervisor, as well as serving as a special helper to the four interns.

The Stanford University five-year program for secondary-school teachers requires an academic major of at least 36 semester hours, a minor of at least 20 hours, a minimum of 40 hours in general education, and a minimum of 22 hours of professional education. The 40 hours in general education must include a minimum of 6 hours each in science and mathematics, practical arts and fine arts, social sciences, and the "communicative" arts. The candidate who completes these requirements satisfactorily is granted a certificate which authorizes him to teach in grades 7 through 14; this authorization is an important factor in California where two-year community junior colleges are springing up like wild flowers.

There is nothing "soft" about the program that future high-school teachers take at Stanford. For instance, although it takes only a "C" average to graduate, it takes a "B—" average to be eligible for the teacher-credential program. The prospective teacher must first complete work for a B.A. degree in the School of Humanities and Science before taking the major portion of his courses in professional education. In addition to satisfying the requirements for a departmental major and related minor, he must also satisfy the requirements for a teaching major and minor. *In many cases, the candidate who has to meet both requirements will have a stronger preparation in his teaching subjects than will the students who are not preparing to teach. Some of the teaching minors, for instance, require three times as many units in academic courses as do departmental minors.*

Although the candidate usually enrolls in the education courses in his fifth year, he is urged to take the professional courses in psychology, sociology, and health education, and in the methods of teaching his minor subject during his junior and senior year, to allow more flexibility in the fifth-year program and to permit him to take some graduate work in his teaching major and minor. *The undergraduate who is a candidate for the secondary teaching credential devotes from 86 to 90 per cent of his program to courses in general studies and in his teaching major or minor. These figures do not include whatever academic electives he may have studied.*

At about the same time the Stanford program was getting underway, a somewhat similar project was becoming firmly established on the East Coast. This is the Master of Arts in Teaching (M.A.T.), a new kind of degree that does not require the professional specialization of the Master of Education, nor the research and academic specialization of the Master of Arts. It is primarily designed for prospective teachers in junior high schools and high schools and contains elements of both the Stanford programs outlined above. The idea was born at Harvard in 1936, and the program has reached its greatest popularity in the so-called Ivy League schools since 1951-52.

Basically, the idea is to recruit the most promising college graduates into the teaching profession. The plan differs in detail from school to school, but in general it works something like this: the graduates are introduced to the teaching profession at special summer schools for junior-high- and senior-high-school students. During the morning they teach classes under the critical eye of experienced teachers and members of their college faculty; in the afternoons they get a stiff dose of professional education. When the regular school year opens, they are placed as interns in the public schools for half the year, and take graduate work in academic subjects and professional education the other half. The M.A.T. is awarded at the end of the public-school year. Sometimes the program calls for two sessions of summer school, and in at least one school it is a full two-year program.

Ernest Stabler, chairman of the M.A.T. program at Wesleyan University, reporting to the American Council on Education, said recently:

Only fragmentary evidence is available, but it is quite clear that M.A.T. graduates tend to stay in teaching. Fewer than 10 per cent of Wesleyan graduates in the past seven years have turned to other careers, and a study of 210 Harvard graduates over a 10-year period reveals that 76 per cent of the men and 62 per cent of the women were still at work in the field of education. These figures are, comparatively speaking, quite remarkable. A study of Illinois graduates who had prepared to teach found that fewer than 10 per cent were teaching 10 years after graduation.[1]

This bears out what many educators have been saying for a long time: if you make the standards high enough, you will attract the most able students and eventually end the teacher shortage.

[1] Ernest Stabler, "The Master of Arts in Teaching Idea," *The Educational Record* 41: 228; July 1960.

CHAPTER ELEVEN

It Takes More Than Talk

No political convention ever elected a president or changed the nation's foreign policy. No pep rally ever won a football game. Science fiction writers have been talking about outer space for years, but they were not the ones who got us there. This is belaboring the obvious, but it is well to remember that all the goals that were set and all the programs that were proposed at Bowling Green, Kansas, and San Diego were just that—goals and proposals. If changes are to be made in teacher education programs, they will not be made in convention assembled. Better teachers can come only from better programs planned on individual college and university campuses. This will be no easy task, however great the cooperation and desire.

The closer the goals and the proposals move toward the campus, the more valuable, the more effective, they become. This was the strength of seven regional conferences held in January, 1960, in Denver, Washington, Reno, Chicago, Louisville, Oklahoma City, and Boston. They were small—ranging from 146 to 298 participants—and they operated outside the limelight of national publicity. But they had the same goal as the national conferences—a better prepared teacher—and they pondered the same questions: how do we produce him, and how should the individual college go about planning programs to this end? The regionals were planned specifically to provide a vigorous follow-up and a wider involvement of educators in the study of the preceding national conference.

The regional conferences built upon the foundations laid at Bowling Green and Kansas, and it should come as a shock to no one that the recommendations made by the study groups fairly well followed the ideas put forth in these two national meetings. But the regionals were *not* miniatures or carbon copies of the nationals, and this is good. The participants were, to coin a cliché, getting "closer to the grass roots," and they sometimes saw things in a different light. Rose-colored glasses are fine for watching sunsets; they are considerably less useful in reading the small print.

At Bowling Green and at Kansas, heavy stress was laid—and quite properly—on the importance of cooperation among the various departments of those colleges and universities with teacher education programs. In the regionals, some concern was expressed that the public schools were being ignored in the planning. The study groups pointed out that the public schools had a responsibility in the recruitment and encouragement of future teachers, and in the supervision of students assigned to them for practice teaching—a responsibility they do not always shoulder in good grace. On the other hand, representatives of the public schools complained that the professors in schools of education had no idea of the problems that classroom teachers face, and showed no desire to find out. This was not a new development, merely a different degree of emphasis. They also said that the same is true of liberal arts professors, except more so.

On a number of points, different study groups tackled the same problems and came up with completely opposite recommendations (just as other study groups had done at the national conferences). One group, for instance, said college students should not be admitted to teacher education programs until their junior year; another group said it just did not make sense to try to recruit students in education, then bar them from education courses for several years. One group urged that every teacher, including those in elementary schools, have an academic major; another said this was *no* answer to any problem.

It was in the regionals that the first real opposition was expressed to the idea of a five-year teacher education program. Some of it was bitter: it was nothing more than a device to fatten the college purse. Some sounded selfish: the fifth year would make the student just that much more attractive to private industry, and he would be lured away from the profession. Some seemed entirely reasonable: it's plain foolishness to rush into a five-year program without first doing everything possible to improve the four-year program.

L. D. Haskew, Dean of the College of Education, University of Texas, made the latter point when he gave the keynote address at the Oklahoma City Regional. He agreed that experimentation with five-year programs should proceed because "there is little doubt that it is possible to use with profit 25 per cent more time in getting students ready to begin teaching." "But," he added, "I am not convinced that the pressure on the four-year programs is as great as some people say."

Haskew said that the demands for 60 semester hours of general education for teachers can be met if some of the academic underbrush is whacked away.

We have hardly scratched the surface yet in eliminating the college semester hours spent in re-runs of high-school material. Better college teaching, realignment of college course content, reassessing credit-hour values, introduction of higher standard expectations—add all of these together and we may recapture 15 to 20 semester hours of course time for the average college student. Efforts in this direction are much more difficult to make than are efforts to get some more time at the top, but shouldn't they precede advocacy of an additional year of college for 100,000 young people every year?

He also warned that rushing into a five-year plan takes the heat off the college planners and puts it on the teaching profession. "We college folks can fold our hands, coo at each other about how wonderful our co-operation is, and wait for the states to enact a five-year certification law."

Haskew wondered, too, whether all those folks issuing "high flown and idealized" statements about what ought to go into teacher education were thinking of the students—"awfully young, awfully immature"—or the experienced, successful, lengthily educated professionals they had observed at work. Is it possible, he asked, that the preparation of beginning teachers not only guarantees the strengths of maturity but also eliminates all weaknesses of age?

A speaker at the Chicago Regional poked a good-sized hole into the argument that teacher education must be improved because the public demands only the best. Said Dean Emerson Shuck of the College of Liberal Arts, Bowling Green State University:

If the primary motive in employing new teachers is to secure a coach who can round out his program with some academic subject, if the school is regarded primarily as a center for community amusement, if the kind of courses the parents demand is the kind that can be passed without effort, if there is too much concern for pure adjustment and too little for intellectual effort, then teachers selected and prepared for quality teaching will go for naught.

If a school is to give priority to intellectual education, Shuck said, the school administration must lead both the public and the student body toward that goal. And he questioned that such leadership was available from administrators who have spent a great deal of their few precious years in preparation for non-intellectual fields, such as coaching athletics or teaching shop. The number of school administrators drawn from these fields is out of proportion to those from other fields taught in either the schools or colleges, Shuck said, and there must be something wrong with the system that permits this.

It is one thing to agree that a teacher needs a broad general education, a study in depth of an academic field, and solid professional education—it is something else again to say just what those things are. Dean Ralph E. Page, of the College of Arts and Sciences of the University of Florida, pointed out to the Louisville Regional that: (1)

at the present time there is no universally acceptable concept of
"general" education; (2) merely setting an arbitrary number of
courses in an academic field will not insure mastery of that subject;
and (3) no specified number of credit hours of professional education
on a college transcript automatically guarantees a good teacher. Yet,
changes must be made, and made soon, for at the traditional rate of
change in education in this country, "our schools in the year 2000 will
be preparing students to meet the needs which are apparent today.
. . . I doubt seriously that we can afford that much delay. By some
means we must accelerate desirable educational changes. Our democratic American society may not be able to exist for another forty
years without such help."

This is not a problem for educators alone. T. M. Stinnett, executive
secretary of the National TEPS Commission, told the regional meetings in Washington, Chicago, and Louisville:

We have so little time; and we have so much time. We have so little
time to overhaul our values, our emphases, and our directions as a people
against the fearsome backdrop of awesome developments in the world.
Yet we have so much time to fritter away as to make the other maddeningly
difficult.

.   .   .

As a nation we seem, momentarily at least, to have lost our way. Here
are some case examples: the sordid revelations of the TV quiz riggings; the
alleged payoffs to disc jockeys to determine what music the American people
will hear; the brazen distortions of the hucksters who consider the nation
a conglomerate mass of 180 million boobs; the creation of synthetic
characters called celebrities who set our values, speech, and fashion for us;
the even more sordid selling of political candidates to the public with the
same techniques employed to market a new dentifrice; our vacillating
foreign policy; our obsession with notoriety and money as a measure of
success, and with abnormal biceps or bosoms as marks of distinction.
Blaring headlines exposing the lavish expenditures by defense-contract
industries to entertain high-ranking defense officials, generals, and admirals
are shrugged off by the average citizen as old stuff. Above all, there appears
to be no overweening sense of any moral goals, no dominating sense of
great purpose by our people—only success and getting ahead as yardsticks.

.   .   .

And besides the skidding values in our society, there is the competitive
threat of Russia. Khrushchev's persistent reiteration of the phrase, "We will
bury you," is one the American people had better not dismiss in anger as
the vapid enunciation of a braggart. Suppose, for example, that Russian
production of consumer goods and standards of living can be brought
abreast of ours in a decade or two decades in the foreseeable future. What
will we then have to [show] . . . the world that constitutes an inviting pre-

eminence? It will no longer be our machines, our imposing automobiles, our technology, our tall buildings, our money, our wealth. Will our material opulence be an adequate counter faith to communism? Will our denunciation of the Russian system as "godless materialism" stand up in the eyes of the rest of the world in the face of much evidence that we, too, have succumbed to a similar doctrine?

An easy answer is that we still have our freedom. Will our freedom be any different? Doubtless the Russians will be free to go to professional games of whatever kind; look at television, at whatever fare the powers-that-be decide is good for the masses. They will be free to go to the beach, or play golf, or watch movies; free to buy on the installment plan; free to hear music which is censored music; free to guzzle beer or vodka or whatever is our guzzling equivalent; free to vote for a candidate that is pre-selected and pre-elected. These are the freedoms which parallel ours in many distressing ways. But what about the larger meaning of freedom? Individuality, for example: the growing image of the organization man and our corporate life are rapidly threatening the elimination of that possibility.

.   .   .

What is the answer, if any, to this spreading debasement, and to our confusion of purpose? There is no point in railing at the increasing complexity of our society or in nostalgic yearning for the simpler ways of yesteryear. The complexity is a fact of life and only the catastrophe of atomic war could decelerate or halt it. . . . By all the signs we can read, in all probability technology will become more complex; automation will grow; cities will multiply and increasingly inundate our rural areas; populations will continue to swell alarmingly, piling one social and economic explosion upon another; the trend toward specialization of endeavor will continue the tragic fragmentation of society; governments and governmental organizations will tend to grow bigger and more stifling of human rights; the cynical manipulations of people will tend to grow more cynical and brutal; the corporate man will likely increasingly replace individual man; the anonymity of the mob will increasingly offer a haven for the frustrated— threatening the eventuality that man the individual will be lost in man the mass; and if this comes to pass, the phrase, "the sanctity of individual human personality," will become just another cliché, and freedom itself will become but an empty word, piously mouthed for the sole purpose of driving the idea from the earth.

But Stinnett spoke not as a prophet of gloom and doom. It is human to accentuate the negative, he said, but "one cannot escape the notion that the American people are neither as degraded nor as hopeless" as they often seem. Above all, he said, "we should talk about these things because man is not yet helpless in these changes—or need not be. He is capable of infinite adaptiveness—and education is the chief adaptive weapon."

Another speaker warned that educators must *not* choose the wrong weapons to fight the good fight for changes in education. Dave Darland, assistant secretary of the National TEPS Commission, told the regional meetings in Denver, Reno, Oklahoma City, and Boston:

(1) Let's not use the single, horrible example to arrive at a false generalization. (2) Let's not over-glorify, underrate, or misrepresent the past. In short, let's not "rig" history. (3) Let's not demand absolute justification of a new idea before raising a finger to change an old pattern. . . . (4) Let's not fall into the opposite extreme of merely changing something just for the sake of change. (5) Let's not be satisfied with minor adjustments where major reformation is needed. (6) And let's not use too much of our valuable energy either to answer or to mimic our critics. (7) Let's not attempt to provide simple answers to complex problems—all panaceas are tyranny in disguise. (8) Let's not forget that the "get-tough" syndrome is silly, but not quite as silly as battling over problems that no longer exist.

Let's *do* have the courage to isolate our problems, establish priorities, and chart our own course, remembering that there is little nobility in being better than someone else, but that true nobility comes in improving ourselves.

CHAPTER TWELVE

Certification—Capstone or Booby Trap?

There are 1,147 colleges and universities in the United States which prepare teachers for our public schools, and some of them do a pretty poor job of it. There are more than 600 different teaching certificates issued in this country, but not one of them can *guarantee* that the holder is a good teacher—any more than a driver's license can *guarantee* that the holder is a safe driver. The certificate does guarantee that the holder has followed a prescribed program of preparation, but this program may be very bad or very good, depending upon the institution. These are the thorny problems of accreditation and certification, and the sad state of their affairs was cussed and discussed, viewed and reviewed, in long and sometimes bitter debate at the San Diego Conference. There was general agreement that something ought to be done, but less than agreement on what that something ought to be.

The professional educators and the liberal arts scholars found a measure of agreement at Bowling Green—a teacher had to know both *what* and *how* to teach. They found further agreement in Kansas on how to put a teacher-education program together. But when they tried, in San Diego, to determine the who's, the what's, and the when's of teacher cerification they asked a lot more questions than they answered.

A certificate is a teacher's license, and in many respects it does not carry the weight and authority of his driver's license. It may mean that the holder has had excellent preparation, or that he may have had none. It may be completely valid in one state, valid with reservations in another, and not worth a hoot in a third. One state issues more than sixty teaching certificates; another issues only one.

The certificate may say the holder is qualified to teach English, although for the past three years he has been teaching mathematics and history—for which he is *not qualified*. Everyone deplores the use of emergency certificates, issued to those who are not fully qualified to teach but who are needed to fill a space in a classroom; yet, the requirements for an emergency certificate in some states are actually higher than for a standard certificate in others.

With a few exceptions, teacher certificates are issued by the various state departments of education. About half the states use the "approved program" approach; that is, after they have approved the teacher-education program in the colleges and universities of their states they will issue certificates to graduates on the recommendation of those schools. In other states, it is largely a matter of counting courses and credit hours to insure that certain requirements have been met. Most of these states, too, require a recommendation from the college or university.

Now, if Americans would just stay put, teacher certification would not be a national problem. If all the graduates of teacher-education institutions would just stay within the boundaries of the state in which they received their preparation to teach, the states could work out their own programs and be satisfied—or stuck—with the teachers produced by those programs. But it does not work out that way. About twelve million Americans move from one state to another every year, including roughly 100,000 teachers. It is more than just a question of itchy feet or the lure of distant climes. California, with the highest teachers' salaries in the nation, actively recruits teachers from all over the country. Ohio meets its shortage by hiring teachers from Kentucky, West Virginia, Pennsylvania, Indiana, Minnesota, and Illinois. Other states follow similar practices, depending on the rewards they can offer.

The solution is obvious, and it sounds easy if you say it fast enough: let us have national standards and just one teaching certificate, good in any school district in any state of the Union. This ideal situation may be achieved some day—there are those who say it *has* to be achieved—but as of right now it seems a long way in the future. Among other things, it means universal adoption of a program of teacher education acceptable in every state, along the lines of the agreements reached at the Kansas Conference. Many of the states will have to toughen up their requirements for a certificate. Hundreds of colleges and universities will have to overhaul and improve their programs to meet the higher standards.

Three states (Arizona, District of Columbia, and California) require a minimum of five years of college preparation for beginning high-school teachers and five other states (Connecticut, Indiana, New York, Oregon, and Washington) require the completion of the fifth year within a specified period of time. Are the rest of the states going to raise their standards this high? Can there be a "national" certificate, when eight states will issue a certificate for teaching in elementary school to someone who has had less than four years of college work?

This is just part of the problem, and it will be dealt with at greater length in a later chapter. But before we try to look any further into the future, let us take a look backward and see where this all began.

Since there was very little in the way of teacher education in the colonial days—at least as we think of it today—there was little in the way of certification. Each community solved its educational needs in its own way. In areas where church influence was strong, a teaching license—if required at all—stressed moral character, religious zeal, and conformity to church doctrine. The first loyalty oath was demanded by the governor of New Jersey, in a proclamation requiring teachers to swear they would not engage in subversive activities against the British Crown. This was also required in other colonies and quite often was more important than anything else in the license. In general, however, the basic requirement of a colonial teacher was the ability to keep order in the classroom; not too much attention was given the question of whether he knew anything at all about the Three R's. There was mobility of teachers in those days, too. A teacher dismissed by one community as drunk, disorderly, dishonest and immoral, or maybe just plain ignorant, had only to hike to the next community to get another job.

Changes in teacher certification were slow to come after America won its independence (although the loyalty oath to the British Crown was followed by one to the United States). Gradually there came a movement toward state supervision of public schools, a movement that began when the states began bearing part of the cost, but it was not until after the Civil War that the authority to issue a certificate began to move slowly from local and county authorities to the states. Really, not until the early 1900's did this shift get underway in earnest. State certificates were issued on the basis of written examinations, usually without regard to the prospective teacher's own education. Even after the turn of the twentieth century the typical examination did not require education beyond the tenth grade, and it was not until 1907 that Indiana became the first state to require a high-school diploma as a condition for all teachers' certificates.

The explosive expansion of American education after 1910 brought new rules and regulations in certification. Before 1900, most states issued a blanket certificate that was good for any subject at any grade level. Only six of the states required a different certificate for elementary- and secondary-school teaching. Gradually there was a move toward special certificates for special teaching assignments. The standards were tightened and graduation from college became more important, even though it was some time before courses in professional education were required.

World War I reversed the trend toward insistence on better teachers and better teaching. A survey by the National Education Association in 1918 showed that half of the teaching force of 600,000 persons had no special professional education, and 100,000 of the total had less than two years of education beyond the eighth grade. In 1921 there were thirty states which had no definite scholarship requirements for a certificate, but by 1926 this number had dropped to fifteen.

With the Depression and general unemployment of the 1930's, there came a surplus of teachers and a continuing rise in minimum standards. It was during this period that the first major demands were made for a five-year college program for teachers. Even so, it is shocking to realize that as recently as 1931 nearly half the states would issue a certificate to a high-school graduate. These graduates—and many of them from poor high schools at that—were given teaching jobs in elementary schools and it is impossible to calculate the damage they were able to do.

Whatever improvements were made during the Depression were virtually wiped out by the effects of World War II. Teachers flocked to war industries and the number of students enrolled in teacher education programs dropped off. A teacher shortage developed that this country has not yet overcome. Because *somebody* had to be in the classroom, emergency or substandard certificates became the order of the day. At the height of the teacher shortage it was estimated that as many as 140,000 teachers held emergency certificates. By 1948 the number was about 101,000 and by 1959 it was 95,700.

But during these postwar years the total number of teachers increased tremendously and there is hope in the fact that while one out of ten teachers held an emergency certificate in the 1949-50 school year, by 1958-59 the ratio had dropped to one out of thirteen. It should be pointed out again that there is no precise or universal definition of an "emergency certificate"; some are better than others, and some are even better than a few standard certificates.

Any history of teacher certification in this country has to be a chronicle of chaos. The situation is better now than ever before, but there is still considerable room for improvement. All the states require a bachelor's degree for a secondary-school certificate. Forty-two of the states require the bachelor's degree for elementary-school teachers, and Missouri adopted the degree minimum effective in the fall of 1961.

One hurdle, more irritating than real, to the free flow of teachers across state lines is the requirement by nine states of special courses which usually can be secured only in an institution within the state. The states, and the special requirements, are as follows:

Arizona, "Constitutions of the United States and Arizona"
Louisiana, "Louisiana History" for upper elementary-grade teachers only

Nevada, "Nevada Constitution and State Law"
Oklahoma, "Oklahoma History"
Rhode Island, "Rhode Island Education," which must be completed
   within three years after the teacher begins teaching in the state
Texas, "Texas and Federal Governments"
Washington, "Washington School Law, History and Government"
Wisconsin, cooperatives and conservation for certain teachers only
Wyoming, "Wyoming Constitution"

The number of such special courses has been declining steadily in recent years, and even where they still exist the regulations have been eased somewhat. For instance, in Nevada, Oklahoma, and Wyoming, the applicant for a certificate is allowed to demonstrate his competence in the special fields by examination instead of being required to take a formal credit course.

In 1959 the states issued a total of 630 different certificates, ranging from one in West Virginia (with one or more forms) to 65 in New Jersey. Of the total, 88 are issued on preparation below the bachelor's degree, 312 require the bachelor's degree, 45 require more than the bachelor's degree but less than five years of college work, 161 require the master's degree, 8 require more than five but less than six years, 10 require six years, and 6 require the doctor's degree.

All this is confusing enough, but there is even more confusion in a discussion of the various types of certificates issued by the states. They fall into three categories.

Life and Permanent Certificates: Twenty-seven states issue this type, and in twenty-six of them it is not permanent at all; it is valid only so long as the holder teaches continuously, or is not out of teaching beyond a specified number of years, or if he completes additional college work. Only in New York does permanent *mean* permanent.

Blanket Certificates: Sixteen states issue these high-school certificates. They do not indicate which fields and subjects the holder is qualified to teach. But they are *not* an authorization to teach in any or all fields, as the name indicates. All states have "teaching field prescriptions" which teachers must meet to be legally assigned to teach a particular field. In some states these prescriptions are set forth in the certification regulations; in some they are given in the accrediting, or "approval" regulations; in Alaska and Colorado the requirements are set forth *both* in certification and in accreditation regulations.

Endorsed Certificates: The most common practice among the states is to issue a certificate which carries an endorsement showing the school level and academic fields or subjects which the holder is qualified to teach. Thirty-seven states endorse the academic field, thirty-one states endorse special fields as well (such as physical education, music, and guidance), and thirteen states issue a separate certificate for each special field.

There was much discussion at the San Diego Conference on the pros and cons of testing in issuing certificates. Sixteen states report some use of testing in certification: Colorado, District of Columbia, Florida, Illinois, Kansas, Maine, Missouri, New Hampshire, New Jersey, New York, Nevada, Oklahoma, South Carolina, Utah, West Virginia, and Wyoming. Only in Missouri is testing used for initial certification, without substantial academic requirements. The county superintendents of schools in Missouri are authorized to give examinations to high-school graduates for elementary-school teaching posts in rural schools. Illinois will issue certificates for elementary-school teachers to persons who have completed two years of college work and who take a qualifying examination. New York uses examinations to certify certain foreign language teachers. Florida uses the National Teacher Examinations to validate the credentials of out-of-state applicants from non-accredited institutions. West Virginia is experimenting with the use of examinations for bachelor's degree holders who lack professional education courses.

In recent years the states have been tightening their requirements for teaching certificates, and this is good. Nebraska, for instance, is raising its minimum requirements toward the bachelor's degree level. Florida has increased the requirements for a major in nearly all fields; South Carolina has increased the minimum requirements in languages; Montana requires 30 semester hours each in chemistry, physics, biology, and general science for full-time teaching, and 20 semester hours for half-time or less, where no specifications were previously listed.

The trend also seems to be to require in the neighborhood of 18 semester hours of professional education for high-school teachers and about 24 hours for elementary-school teachers. Remember, however, that we are talking here about state requirements—not about what the teacher education institution might require or make available.

There is a great, and often discouraging, variation in the number of semester hours required in the academic fields for teachers' certificates. Among the various states the range in English, for instance, is from 12 to 40 semester hours, with the median at 24 hours. (For the non-mathematical, the "median" is the numerical middle, or halfway point, meaning there are as many figures above it as below it— it is *not* an average.) In other subjects the range and the median are:

Subject	Range	Median
Modern languages	12-42	20
Mathematics	12-40	18
Chemistry	12-40	17

Subject	Range	Median
Physics	8-40	17
Biology	8-30	18
General science	12-40	18
Social science	12-48	24
Science	12-48	24
Physical science	8-40	16
Biological sciences	12-40	18

It is nice to think about the day when all the states will have the same number and kind of teaching certificates, and the same standards for acquiring them. But until the states, working closely with the professional educators and the liberal arts scholars, agree on common goals and common pathways to those goals, "national certification" will remain a dreamlike, Utopian thing always out of reach.

CHAPTER THIRTEEN

Flexibility Without Laxity

The primary purpose of teacher certification is, and always has been, to protect children from incompetent teachers. But the same high standards and rigid regulations which are supposed to bar the schoolhouse door to the poor teacher can also keep out some good ones. This is a point on which certification is most often attacked, as in a *Saturday Evening Post* editorial of July 19, 1958, entitled, "They Wouldn't Let Beethoven Teach Music in Indiana." A more frequently cited charge is that Einstein would not be allowed to teach high-school mathematics because he had never taken any courses in professional education. Now these are eye-catching declarations, and there is enough truth in them to point up a real problem. They do, of course, overlook three important things: (1) in all probability, neither would have considered for a moment becoming a high-school teacher; (2) it just may be that both Einstein and Beethoven would have been *poor* teachers; and (3) there probably is not a school district in the country which would not have found *some way* to get them certificates if they were available as teachers.

Paul Woodring of the Fund for the Advancement of Education, had this to say about it at the San Diego Conference:

When it has been charged that present certification requirements would prohibit a Toscanini from teaching music in high school or an Einstein from teaching mathematics, the conventional reply has been that they should be excluded because these men would not understand adolescents and would be unable to adapt their teaching to the less able students. This is not a very good reply. It may be true, but we have no way of knowing that it is. We do know that Harvey White is a very able teacher of high-school physics, that Robert Frost and Carl Sandburg can arouse an interest in poetry on the part of young people, and that Leonard Bernstein is a superb teacher of music to people of all ages. None of these could meet rigid certification requirements, but we know that they are good teachers because we have seen them teach and have watched students respond to their teaching. If we insist that they are not qualified or that they do not understand young people, we only make our position ridiculous.

It is not likely that such men will ever want to teach in a self-contained classroom where they would be required to keep records, take off overshoes, and collect the milk money. But as members of a teaching team, perhaps as television instructors, we can use them and ought to use them. Their presence among us will do far more to exalt our ranks than we can hope to achieve by any efforts to build high walls around our profession. Teachers should be held to high standards, but these should not be confused with technical requirements and rigid rules. We still know all too little about what courses and what experiences make the difference between a great teacher and a mediocre one. Until we find out, teaching should remain an open and flexible, not a closed and rigid profession.

What confuses the issue is that these arguments are not really about the Einsteins, the Beethovens, and the Toscaninis at all. They really concern the college graduate with a liberal arts degree—but no education courses—who decides to become a teacher. She may be a housewife who has raised a family and believes her experience fits her for the classroom. He may be a military officer in retirement. He may be a student who does not realize until he has his B.A. degree in hand that teaching is what he always wanted to do. He may be a teacher from France who wants to teach French in elementary school but cannot be certified on the basis of his college transcript.

Certainly the door to teaching should not be slammed in the face of these people if they have the makings of good teachers. Just as certainly, motherhood alone does not qualify a woman as a teacher, nor is the command of a regiment all the background a man needs before stepping into a classroom. What is needed, it was almost unanimously agreed at San Diego, is flexibility, and "flexibility" was the most used and abused word in that conference. One speaker defined it this way: "Make an exception in my case, but hold everyone else to rigid standards." The big problem here is to find the means of admitting to the profession the competent deviate, without opening the gates to a flood of incompetents. This is not an easy problem for which there are simple, clear-cut, and definitive solutions.

Dean Emerson Shuck of the College of Liberal Arts, Bowling Green (Ohio) State University, voiced an ardent plea for flexibility, after first warning that the minimum standards of certification should never become the maximum standards for judging the qualifications of teachers. Speaking of the mature persons who want to enter the profession late in life (such as the housewife whose family has grown up), Shuck said:

This group constitutes a source of wisdom, balance, and potential dedication which our schools can use happily. . . . At the same time, they are independent enough to choose whether they will spend several summers or a year taking courses designed for late adolescents, in order to be permitted to enter a classroom. Often they will simply give up in disgust.

Of those with special talents to offer, such as retired officers, accountants, or engineers who might be willing to teach mathematics (and do a better job of it than a fully certified person who had barely completed a college minor in mathematics), Shuck said, "I feel that such people would take their responsibilities seriously enough to learn a great deal about the art of teaching; but like the previous group, they cannot or will not pursue formal course work to meet such a requirement."

The responsibility lies squarely on the teaching profession, Shuck said, to take the initiative; to screen such candidates, assist them, and evaluate them courageously. He suggested, as one method of extending certification to such candidates, the use of proficiency examinations plus personal screening and a supervised teaching experience.

Woodring spoke specifically of the liberal arts student who makes a late decision to go into teaching.

By the time he is a college senior, teaching looks much more attractive . . . than it did when he left high school, and some very able candidates will be lost to the profession if we fail to make provision for the bright liberal arts student who makes the decision to teach near the end of his undergraduate career. For such people, fifth-year programs are essential and they must be made attractive to highly intelligent, liberally educated people. If the liberal arts graduate is looked upon as a "retread" and is required to take professional courses designed for freshmen or sophomores, he will not become a teacher. But we cannot afford to lose him. We need programs especially tailored to the student who already has a knowledge of philosophy, history, and the behavioral sciences, and which build upon it. Most of our existing introductory courses in education are not so designed.

It was not to be expected that everyone at San Diego would agree with Shuck or Woodring. C. O. Wright, executive secretary of the Kansas State Teachers Association, listened to Shuck and then asked: "Are we talking about flexibility or laxity? I disagree with the dean on most of his points. I would throw out his gimmicks, set up a required five-year program with no exceptions and let the flexibility be within the colleges." Proficiency examinations for teachers? "Nonsense," said Wright. "They do little but prove you can take a test."

Earl E. Mosier, assistant commissioner for higher education in New Jersey, was another who had harsh words for proficiency examinations for would-be teachers. In one of the conference working papers, Mosier declared we are suffering nationally from an overdose of testing.

Those who would grant teaching certificates on the basis of performance on a test or a battery of tests fail to weigh carefully the fact that the evaluation of teacher effectiveness involves a consideration of individual attitudes, knowledge, skills, values, and emotional stability, among many other factors.

Teaching is not something . . . to be acquired by experience as a student. Having attended school is not in itself sufficient preparation to teach. There is little more logic to such a position than there would be to saying that having gone shopping all our lives is the only necessary preparation for running a supermarket, or having driven a car qualifies the driver to repair his own or design next year's model.

If an individual is not willing to complete the necessary program of professional education to qualify for a teaching position, then he does not and should not qualify to enter the profession.

Jay E. Greene of the New York City Board of Examiners agreed with Mosier that there is no written test now available, or in sight, that can accurately measure all the complex factors that make up teacher competence. But he proposed that all teacher candidates be given examinations *after* they have completed their programs of preparation and have been recommended by their institutions, but *before* they are issued certificates. These examinations would test the candidate's knowledge in his academic field, such as science, foreign language, or English, and in his professional field, such as methods of teaching or child psychology. Students may take these courses, receive passing grades in them, and go into teaching without ever having achieved a reasonable mastery in them, Greene said.

In a conference working paper, he told of academic specialty tests given in New York City to applicants for high-school teaching certificates who had been prepared in accredited teacher education institutions in various parts of the country. For instance, of the 370 prospective teachers who took the test in social studies, the range of individual ratings was from 82 per cent to 20 per cent; fifty-two applicants were below 40 per cent and ten were below 30 per cent. The test for English majors was taken by 281 candidates, whose ratings ranged from 90 to 30 per cent; twenty-nine rated below 50 per cent and eight below 40 per cent. Results in the field of mathematics were poorest, Greene said. The math test was taken by 192 candidates; three received more than 90 per cent but forty had marks below 25 per cent. Tests of ability to write reasonably correct English showed that about ten out of every 100 applicants would not meet a minimum standard. The examinations in professional background knowledge and understanding also revealed a disturbing number who did not have a reasonable mastery, Greene said.

In general, the discussion groups at San Diego were all in favor of flexibility—providing it did not mean expediency, loopholes, laxity, or "just making exceptions." One group, for instance, agreed that "flexibility should *not* be construed to permit persons with inadequate preparation to 'practice' on children." And the same group declared, "Certification should not be set up in too rigid a fashion, because we do not know enough about teaching and learning to be dogmatic about the specific ingredients of programs of preparation." Several groups pointed out that *rigor mortis* of the certificate sets in when it is choked to death with the red tape of strict requirements in courses and credit hours. They asked state certification officials to work toward the abolition of such one-state-only courses as state history. Other groups expressed approval of experimentation in alternate programs of certification, such as the proficiency examinations, periods of internship, and the like.

There was general dissatisfaction with the current practice in many states of trying to determine the ability and competence of a teacher by adding up a row of courses and credit hours and checking them off against some sort of a master plan. This is hardly surprising since 40 per cent of the participants in the San Diego Conference were classroom teachers, the ones most harmed and irritated by such bookkeeping. One group put it this way:

Certification requirements should be written in terms of general areas and levels of preparation rather than in terms of specific courses and semester-hour requirements. They should simply insure that institutional programs have the necessary ingredients described in broad terms.

And how about the near-Einsteins, the almost-Toscaninis, and the Johnny-come-latelys? Most of the conference participants seemed to agree they would make welcome additions to the teaching profession and efforts should be made to make them *eligible* for certification, possibly through special examinations, supervised teaching, or short but intense courses in professional education. There is an important distinction between making someone eligible for certification, and granting him a certificate outright, as witness these excerpts from the discussion group reports.

Intelligent, mature people with a desire to teach are *not* acceptable by virtue of this fact alone without proceeding to obtain preparation for teaching. Returnees to teaching should be provided orientation to current programs and some form of practice teaching under close supervision.

·   ·   ·

Parenthood, maturity, experience in the armed forces, etc., should not be accepted in lieu of the completion of an approved program in teacher education in an accredited school.

·   ·   ·

It should be possible to certify qualified candidates who have demonstrated a proficiency in various fields but who have not been certified. However, this should not lead to displacing or handicapping those who have been regularly certified or to a lowering of standards for certification.

What it all boiled down to was recognition of the fact that you cannot dig dandelions with a steam shovel, and you cannot use teacher certification as an educational scalpel. Dean L. D. Haskew of the College of Education, University of Texas, put it all in focus when he told the conference:

Certification is a mass instrument, not a precision tool. It deals most successfully with total populations, total configurations, total levels. Success goes down in direct proportion to its attempts to deal with individuals, with specifics, with exceptions. . . .

Certification is kept vital and constructive by the spirit, not the letter, of the law. Therefore, those procedures which rely as much as possible upon the cultivation of the spirit are most likely to succeed; those which add jots and tittles to the law are most likely to fail.

Certification is a weak tool when used alone, and when used for purposes for which it is unsuited. Certification is at its best when it is an integral part of a trilogy composed of accreditation of institutions of teacher education, teacher education itself, and certification.

. . .

Certification is a weak reed with which to prop up incompetent or indifferent employers. In the long run, a certificate can never substitute for constructive and intelligent personnel policies at the local district level, and we would be much better off if we worked on those policies rather than upon attempted substitutes through the force of certification.

CHAPTER FOURTEEN

Liberty Without License

You would not ask a dentist to remove your appendix. You would not let a blacksmith fix your fine Swiss watch. Chances are, however, you are not nearly so discriminating in the education of your children. Now these are harsh words, and millions of parents can rightfully protest, "Why, I demand nothing but the best for my children's education." The trouble is, you may be demanding more than the schools can supply, particularly in the way of good teachers. Let us consider the situation in foreign languages, as set forth by Dean Elton Hocking of the foreign language department at Purdue University.

"More than 800,000 children are getting regular instruction in a foreign language this year," Hocking told a discussion group at the San Diego Conference. He added:

Obviously, many of these children are getting substandard instruction because their teachers aren't properly prepared. Poor instruction is worse than no instruction at all. If the teaching is inadequate, the program should never be started.

But the movement has caught fire nationally. *There is tremendous pressure on the schools from parents and from parent-teacher organizations.* And the entire program may just collapse some day because of inadequate results.

The same public pressures are applied in other areas—in demands for more physics, more chemistry, more mathematics—and the demand is outrunning the supply. The result, in all too many cases, is the misassignment or malassignment of teachers—giving them jobs they are not prepared to do. The very parents who are demanding nothing but the best for their children may be getting nothing better than the worst.

J. Paul Reynolds, Dean of the College of Arts and Sciences, Florida State University, told of a school principal who could not find a teacher for a French class, and finally decided he would have to teach it himself. A friend of Reynolds' was visiting the school and was invited to pay the class a visit. She took her seat in the back of the room and soon the principal entered, asking the class, *"Părles̱ vŏws Frances̱?"* And the reply came back in unison, *"o͞oy̆, o͞oy̆."*

The situation is particularly bad in the thousands of high schools across the country which are too small to employ enough teachers to teach every subject the way that subject should be taught. A high school with only three or four teachers, for instance, will have to ask those teachers to double up in their subjects. Thus you get a history teacher taking on a class in English, a coach teaching physics, and a math teacher instructing a class in social science.

It is impossible to assess the harm that is done to the students. Some teachers may be able to do more than just a passing job in a field outside their specialty, but the risk is great. A student who learns poor pronunciation of a foreign language is forever handicapped in learning the language. An incompetent teacher can make science and math courses so dull, so frustrating, so uninviting, that many a boy may give up his goal of going into science or engineering. A poorly taught course in high-school chemistry may turn a girl away from a hoped-for career in nursing or medicine.

Several of the San Diego participants declared that the misassignment of teachers is not as widespread as is often charged; but, as one said, "The examples we do see are often so horrendous they are blown up all out of proportion."

The problem is more than just asking a teacher to teach something he knows nothing about. There is the question of whether the teacher is working with the *types of pupils* which he is most capable of teaching. Some teachers do their best work with slow learners, or with those from slum areas or perhaps from broken homes. Others are best with the bright students who are capable of much more work than the average.

Still another aspect, although it is not really misassignment, is illustrated in a story told by Dr. John P. Latimer, Assistant Dean of Faculties at George Washington University. Latimer told of two language teachers he knew. One was an expert in Latin, but also taught German. The other, in a high school eight miles away but in the same city, was an expert in German, but also taught Latin:

I asked one school official why those two teachers didn't teach their specialties at both schools, driving back and forth by car. Then the students at both schools would get the best possible instruction in both languages. I was told it was "absolutely impossible." The reason: the principals of the two schools would lose some measure of control over these teachers. I think this is absurd.

The misassignment of teachers is a problem primarily at the high-school level. The abuses are not so acute in the elementary school because the depth of preparation in a subject-matter field is not so important—except, of course, in the case of foreign languages.

So how does the teaching profession cope with misassignment? Two approaches were suggested at the San Diego Conference.

Robert N. Bush, professor of education at Stanford University, put it squarely up to the teacher himself:

> Each teacher must be so prepared and so firmly imbued with a code of ethics which states that he will not go outside his field of competence in teaching, that he will firmly resist attempts by administrators or the community to force him to teach where he is not prepared. The teacher is the one who must make the critical judgment at the time and the place his assignment is made.

Bush acknowledged that the teacher cannot stand alone in resisting the forces that push him to work outside the field of his competence. He called for a strong tradition of high standards of professional conduct, a tradition so strong that the teacher who later becomes a school administrator will understand that it is unethical to assign a teacher to teach where he is unprepared. Bush also called upon the organized profession to take a strong stand.

> The local organization of teachers, supported by strong regional, state, and national associations, must stand ready to enforce a high code of ethics, a code which contains the provision that teachers shall not be assigned to teach outside their fields of competence.

Bush asked a question which many people concerned with education have asked, without finding a completely suitable answer: Should courses in physics and foreign languages, for instance, be offered in the schools even if no fully qualified teachers are available? Much depends on the size and location of the school and the level of preparation of the teachers available. It might be possible, Bush pointed out, to enlarge existing classes, or to let a mature, experienced teacher supervise the students as they take a correspondence course or pursue the subject through independent study.

"In any particular instance," he said, "the decision as to which line to follow is a complicated and delicate task. *It should be made on the basis of what is best for the pupil.*"

A different approach was suggested by Wayland W. Osborn, Director of the Division of Teacher Education and Certification, Iowa State Department of Public Instruction. Osborn outlined the procedure used in Iowa, whereby the State Department of Public Instruction withholds approval, or accreditation, from a school where misassignments are made.

Sometimes temporary approval is granted where the teacher has had some preparation in a subject-matter area, and agrees to complete appropriate work to remove the deficiency. Teachers found to have no preparation in an area are not given approval, *even if the school is required to drop the course involved.*

The withholding of approval is a potent weapon in fighting misassignments. Most colleges require that applicants for enrollment shall be graduates of approved schools, and Iowa is one of the states in which failure to gain approval means loss of state financial aid. These reasons, plus the matter of local pride, provide a powerful incentive for local school administrators to assign teachers in accordance with their fields of preparation.

Iowa uses the "approved program" approach to teacher education and certification. After the State Board of Public Instruction approves the program of any college or university, the students who complete that course and are recommended by the institution receive general certificates for high-school teaching. Such students also are given *approval statements* to indicate which subjects they may teach with the approval of the Iowa State Department of Public Instruction. Other subjects may be added to this statement as the teacher qualifies. The standards for the certificate and the approval statement may never be lower than the state standards but, depending on the school, they may be considerably higher. The certificate is the holder's license to teach, and the holder may legally teach any subject he has the courage to tackle; similarly it would be perfectly legal for a high school to assign its teachers without regard to the approval statement. It would then, of course, have to face the consequences mentioned above—the loss of approval, or accreditation.

To make sure there are no misassignments in Iowa high schools, the local superintendents of schools file a report each September showing each teacher's assignment. These are put on punch cards, and an electronic business machine is used to compare these cards with punched cards already on file in the department. When misassignments show up, the local superintendent is contacted, and the assignment is changed, or given temporary approval, or approval is withdrawn as described above. If anyone, in or out of the teaching profession, wants to check up on possible misassignments, he need only check in the office of the local superintendent or the county superintendent where, by law, the certificate and the approval statement are recorded. A final note: the county superintendents of schools are required by law to force all public-school teachers without registered certificates to stop teaching.

Many of the discussion groups took note of the misassignment situation, and all were against it. The strongest statement came from a group which proposed that accreditation and state aid should be withheld from the offending school, that the school administration should refuse to offer a course unless it had a properly prepared teacher, that the teacher himself should refuse to teach the course if he is not qualified, and that educational agencies should serve as watchdogs to publicize the misassignment.

Several agreed with Bush that the teacher was the first line of defense against misassignment, but pointed out that younger teachers in particular might not be able to withstand the pressure which could be applied by a school administrator; such teachers should have the entire profession standing behind them. Others made the point that, if the school refused to offer the course without a qualified teacher, this might lead to consolidation and reorganization of the small school districts where the problem is particularly acute. There also was acknowledgment that the primary reason for misassignment is the teacher shortage. Several groups said it might be absolutely necessary for a year, in which case the misassigned teacher should try to qualify himself as quickly as possible, and wherever possible work closely with qualified teachers in the same school.

Strangely enough, not one of the groups even mentioned an appeal to the parents of the children involved, the parents who say they want only the best, but, however unknowingly, often settle for much less.

CHAPTER FIFTEEN

Statesmanship to Fiasco?

The Council for Basic Education, one of the most severe and articulate critics of teacher education in this country, reported on the first of the three cooperative approach conferences under the head-line, "Statesmanship at Bowling Green." Two years later its headline over the story of the third conference was "Fiasco at San Diego." Things had gone to pot, according to Earle Davis, head of the Department of English, Kansas State University, who attended the San Diego Conference as a representative of the American Council of Learned Societies. Davis found nothing to praise but much to criticize: the "old guard" was back in charge; no measure to correct things in *any* area (italics his) was seriously supported; the positive results at San Diego were nonexistent; and "those of us who are devoted to the survival of the basic disciplines should gird our loins and return to the cudgels."

Davis reported on the San Diego Conference as he saw it, which he had the right—indeed, the obligation—to do. This writer was there as a newspaperman and saw things in a considerably different light. There is no desire here to engage in debate with Dr. Davis, but some comments on his comments, which follow, might be in order.

Here is what happened. At Bowling Green most of us were optimistic. We listened to several deans of education, like Dean Stiles of Wisconsin, who represented such forceful and reasonable approaches to teacher training that we all felt invigorated. Give us men like these and where were our problems? Then we went to Lawrence, and some of the same fervor was still in evidence. Educationists seemed to be making many concessions in the direction of more subject-matter requirements, some balance between professional education and serious knowledge, between real knowledge and methodology. Then we went to San Diego. This was the conference where the enacting clause was supposed to be joined to the original recommendations. But by this time the old guard was back in charge.

Any individual reaction to this last conference must be partially dependent on the particular discussion section one happened to be in. (The professional educators always outnumbered the non-professionals ten to one.) My group confined itself to meaningless generalities, refused to meet any issues directly, and there was evident feeling that everything would be fine if people like me did not keep asking for some particular recommendation about the reforms needed in teacher certification.

Early in the conference I decided to try to push a specific proposal in my section as a kind of test case. The measure I chose was the suggestion originally made by Dean Stiles that certification procedures be liberalized by setting up three alternative roads to the goal of competent teaching. A teacher can be certified as at present; or by getting sufficient professional education hours by successfully passing examinations without taking the courses; or by an internship where the candidate is given temporary certification for a year under the guidance of an experienced teacher, who may then at the end of the year recommend permanent certification without further education courses. Something of this kind was envisaged in the excellent speech Dean Emerson Shuck of Bowling Green State University made at the start of the conference sessions, and which we all saw and heard discussed over the closed-circuit TV in each group meeting.

This was supposed to give point to the group discussions, but our group immediately ignored the speech and started talking other issues. Examination of the reports from most groups would indicate that this happened almost everywhere. Several sections finally said that they were in favor of different paths to certification, although nothing specific needed to be done on a national scale. In reply to my advocacy of the Stiles plan, the certification experts pointed out that all this was a fad and that it wasn't working in Wisconsin anyway. The plain fact is that a majority of states would violently oppose (particularly in the education-controlled advisory councils) any shift in their certification procedures. In my own state there has been no single change in liberalizing teacher training certification since the Bowling Green Conference. Mr. C. O. Wright, head of the Kansas State Teachers Association, on one TV panel pointed out that he was satisfied with certification as it is now, and that he was particularly opposed to special examinations. The fact is that no measure to correct things in *any* area was seriously supported in this Conference.

Those professional educators with an honest desire for partnership with the representatives of the basic disciplines exerted less influence at San Diego than at the former conferences. The voice of the basic disciplines was heard less than on the former occasions. . . .[1]

Perhaps the key to Dr. Davis' complaints is to be found in the second paragraph of the quoted material—the discussion group to which he was assigned. (I resist the temptation to debate the first paragraph on the issue of whether there may not be serious knowledge in a good course in the psychology of education.) A few of the groups *were* pretty bad, and I had the advantage over Dr. Davis—he was stuck with one group, but I could, and did, walk out on a couple of them, including the group which decided that the primary justifica-

[1] Earle Davis, "Fiasco at San Diego," Council for Basic Education *Bulletin* 5: 1-2; September 1960.

tion of certification is "a desire to reward those who complete a prescribed training program." And perhaps it only *appeared* to Dr. Davis that he was outnumbered ten to one. The liberal arts scholars actually made up 20 per cent of the conference roster.

If Dr. Davis' group ignored the speech by Emerson Shuck, that certainly did not happen "almost everywhere." Eighteen of the forty discussion groups reported they had considered alternate roads to certification, and it is at least possible that other groups failed to report similar discussions because they failed to reach agreement. It is true enough that there was no overwhelming enthusiasm for adopting the examination-internship methods of certification outright, but there was virtually unanimous agreement in the eighteen groups reporting that further experimentation was needed. This may have been disappointing to Dr. Davis, but it could hardly have been surprising that the teaching profession views with misgivings anything that smacks of lowering the requirements for a certificate that many have worked hard to earn.

These sample comments from the official group reports indicate the general feeling.

We approve experimentation in alternate certification programs such as proficiency examinations and internships.

Efforts should be made to make those with special competences—rich liberal arts backgrounds, for example—eligible for certification as expeditiously as possible. Here, special examinations, a review of non-certificated teaching experiences, etc., might well be employed.

We recommend that the use of nation-wide examinations for teachers be explored as one of several means of evaluating the readiness and competence of prospective teachers.

Flexibility in certification should provide for the recognition of outstanding qualifications and abilities, and the encouragement of experimentation in teacher-education programs. It should prevent the loss of valuable additions to the profession. . . .

Some provision should also be made for determining eligibility for certification among those whose formal deficiencies are in areas other than subject matter.

A variety of ways of attaining certification should be possible.

Institutions should be encouraged to experiment with varying programs and with tests and other procedures for determining the equivalent training and experience for those with unusual backgrounds . . . no demonstrably capable teacher should be barred from teaching by (1) a lack of formal preparation, or (2) individual differences in the pattern of preparation . . .

increased flexibility will be achieved by the greater use of comprehensive examinations.

The more cautious or conservative viewpoint showed up in comments such as the following:

Flexibility of certification should make it possible to certify qualified candidates who have demonstrated a proficiency in various fields but who have not been certified. However, this should not lead to displacing or handicapping those who have been regularly certified, *or to a lowering of standards for certification*. With all of its faults, certification remains the best available means of forecasting competence in the classroom.

The group could not agree as to whether or not examinations could serve as an acceptable substitute for required courses for individuals who appear to have the required knowledge but lack the technical requirements for certification.

The principle that demonstrated proficiency to teach be recognized no matter how acquired and that qualifications be stated as much as possible in terms of demonstrated proficiency should be considered. This is not to be construed as eliminating credit hours, degrees, or approved programs, but rather as placing the emphasis where it belongs—that is, on proficiency.

The art of examination for competency in the teaching profession needs further development before it can be dependable.

Several of the groups took distinct issue with the involved and complex certification requirements now found in some states. One suggested that full credit courses are not really needed in such subjects as state law, state history, audio-visual services, and the like. These courses, the group suggested, might be combined, might be passed by examination, or might be mastered on the job. Another said, "We agreed that there is unnecessary duplication and repetition in courses. Much that is now of classroom concern might better be done elsewhere or completely eliminated from the curriculum." Still another said, without elaboration, "It was agreed there were a significant number of colleges whose training programs for teachers were inadequate, with a resulting number of substandard teachers."

It seems evident that the "old guard" was not in charge of the discussion group which reported:

The composition of the board or bureau that establishes or recommends the particular requirements (for certification) should be examined critically. There should be a definite amount of professional experience represented in such a body, but complete control by people in the profession could easily lead to a blind and unresponsive professionalism.

This comment was made in regard to a proposal circulated to conference participants by Leon W. Cohen, a professor of mathematics at the University of Maryland, "for an informal group of academic people at the conference." Cohen proposed that, to bring the certification requirements of the fifty states more clearly into line, the states establish by law an "advisory council" to assist the state certification officer on "policies and principles of certification." Council membership would be determined by law "so that it represents the several fields of learning such as English, modern languages, classical languages, history, mathematics, physics, chemistry, etc., and the several professional education groups such as classroom teachers, school administrators, professors of education, etc."

All the groups that mentioned the Cohen proposal in their reports approved of it in principle, although nearly all of them made minor changes in the wording, and there was some objection to the provision that it be carried out by passing laws. Other groups worked the same sort of proposal into their reported agreements without mentioning Cohen directly.

If I had interviewed Dr. Davis at San Diego—and I wish I had—I might not be so optimistic about what I personally found there. The liberal arts scholars I talked to in the discussion groups, over coffee, and in the corridors all felt that much good had been done and that the future promised even more progress. One in particular, a professor of philosophy, said, according to my notes, "There isn't any question but what the cooperation between the two groups will continue—that is taken for granted. We have come a very long way since the summer of 1958."

But perhaps both Dr. Davis and I are beating a dead horse. The group reports in any and all of the three conferences are not worth the paper they were written on if they are not followed by constructive action on the campuses of the colleges and universities and in the various state certification offices.

Just one last bit of optimism: there seemed to be general agreement at San Diego that the "approved-program" plan was the best one to follow in up-grading teacher certification. State officials would approve the teacher education program of each college and university within the state, and accept for certification anyone who completes that program and is recommended by the institution. Each institution would be free, of course, to raise its standards at any time by strengthening its teacher education program and this, in effect, would raise the requirements for a certificate. It is on each individual campus that the liberal arts scholars have their best opportunity to make their voices heard. It is there that their views carry the most weight; it is there that they can do the most good.

CHAPTER SIXTEEN

"To Be or Not to Be—Accredited"

The national conferences at Bowling Green, Kansas, and San Diego, plus the seven regional meetings, constituted a sort of "Do-it-yourself Flexner Kit." It was Abraham Flexner who, a half century ago, took a long, hard look at medical education in this country and found it very bad indeed. His study, sponsored by the Carnegie Foundation, was a turning point in medical education. He recommended that 70 per cent of the medical schools be eliminated because of their poor programs and inadequate facilities, that the entire curriculum be overhauled, and that there be a drastic upgrading of admission standards for students. Many medical schools had no laboratories, the teaching was terrible, and the courses were weak. Some of the medical schools were nothing more than diploma mills which accepted any student, regardless of his previous education or his aptitude for medicine—but with high regard for his financial status—and later turned him out to practice on an unsuspecting but suffering public.

Perhaps teacher education has never been in the same sad shape that medical education was when Flexner began investigating, and even the mention of his report may serve to invite an unfair comparison. But there is *one* valid point of similarity: the Flexner report was based on a conception of what the medical profession ought to be and what society had a right to demand that it should be; the national and regional TEPS conferences were an attempt by the nation's educators to determine what the teaching profession ought to be, and what society had a right to demand that it should be.

That is why the thorny problem of "accreditation" kept popping up, particularly at San Diego. Accreditation is the process of setting standards for various programs of education such as medicine, dentistry, law, and education, and then accrediting, or "approving," the institutions that meet those standards. It is a process peculiar to this country; foreigners have a great deal of difficulty understanding it and so, it would appear, do many Americans.

Of all the major nations in the world, only the United States does not have a federal ministry of education to control and supervise the schools from first grade through college. Instead, the fifty individual states have assumed that responsibility—a responsibility they take quite seriously when it comes to elementary and secondary schools, but much less seriously when dealing with colleges and universities. To a degree unknown anywhere else in the world, this country's institutions of higher learning run their own affairs with a minimum of governmental control.

This situation is often an open invitation to abuse, as witness the great number of diploma mills and phony vocational training schools that sprang up after World War II when the federal government began underwriting the education of veterans through the GI Bill. In a tragic number of cases the veterans were enrolled, "trained" or "educated," and graduated with some sort of "degree" without ever once attending a class or opening a book.

When you visit your doctor you know that the license to practice which hangs in his reception room is a guarantee that he is a thoroughly trained professional and not a quack. Before he could take the state examination which led to that license, he was graduated from an *accredited* medical school—one whose program and facilities met the rigid standards of the American Medical Association. Your attorney was graduated from a school accredited by the American Bar Association; your dentist from a dental school accredited by the American Dental Association.

It is reassuring to know that you can entrust your upset stomach, your lawsuits, and your aching cavities to doctors, lawyers, and dentists who have been graduated from accredited institutions. The public deserves, and has the right to demand, the protection from fakes and phonies that the process of accreditation is designed to provide.

Unfortunately, you do not have the same guarantee of high-standard, professional training and education when you entrust your children to the teachers whose job it is to develop each young mind to its full potential.

There *is* an accrediting agency for the teaching profession—the National Council for Accreditation of Teacher Education. Its self-assigned goal is the same as that of the other accrediting agencies: to raise the standards of education and preparation, and to recognize the institutions that meet those standards. Its nineteen members include three collegiate representatives appointed by the National Commission on Accrediting (which is an agency to accredit the accrediting agencies); seven collegiate members appointed by the American Association of Colleges for Teacher Education (NEA); one representative of the Council of Chief State School Officers (state superintendents or commissioners of education); one representative of the National Association of State Directors of Teacher Education and Certification; six representatives of the teaching profession at large, nominated by the National TEPS Commission and appointed by the Executive Committee of NEA; and one representative of the National School Boards Association.

As yet the NCATE has failed to win the approval of the vast army of liberal arts scholars, those very same academicians who have been most bitterly critical of teacher education standards and practices in this country. At the time of the San Diego Conference, only 336 of the 1,147 teacher education institutions in the United States had been accredited by the NCATE. This certainly is not to say that many others could not meet NCATE standards. The NCATE, with its small staff and resources, simply has not yet had time to process all the applications for accreditation, and many colleges simply do not want to submit their programs and facilities to the appraisal of an agency made up primarily of professional educators. Although the NCATE was approved in 1956 by the National Commission on Accrediting and although its structure has been changed to meet the objections of the liberal arts proponents, that group still tends to be skeptical of the NCATE.

The differing views of the NCATE were discussed frequently at San Diego because accreditation and certification are so closely linked that it is difficult to discuss one without mentioning the other. The NCATE was mentioned most frequently by those discussion groups which took up the question of reciprocity among the states in teacher education. (Reciprocity as used here means an agreement that a teacher's certificate granted in one state should be recognized as valid in all other states.) There was general agreement that there can be no national reciprocity until there is national accreditation.

It was the consensus in one group, for instance, that "the continued growth and acceptance of the NCATE program is one of the most significant developments of the present era and should be given the wholehearted support of the teaching profession." But one member of the group filed a minority report in which he declared, "I do not approve of the authority of the NCATE to accredit education schools unless it is reorganized to have much more academic representation." The lack of academic representation on the NCATE was the one big objection raised about it at San Diego.

This seems reasonable enough; if the total profession, the total university, is to be involved in teacher education (already agreed), then the academic scholars should have a voice in the NCATE. Why do they not have that representation? Perhaps the answer is to be found in one of the conference working papers, prepared by William K. Selden, executive secretary of the National Commission on Accrediting. In describing the history of the NCATE Selden wrote:

It might be emphasized that official participation of the Association of American Colleges was sought in order to include direct representation of the liberal arts colleges. This attempt, however, which has been repeated several times, has been unsuccessful for three reasons.

In the first place, the liberal arts people, at least up until a few years ago, frequently objected to the argument that teaching is a profession like medicine or law. For one group of teachers to claim that teaching is not a profession is to proclaim a denial of their own birthright. Teaching shares an ancient heritage of professional status with theology, law, and medicine. Even though teaching in this country does not presently enjoy the preferred economic or social status of law or medicine, the facts of contemporary political life are clear that without an organized presentation of professional goals, improved social and economic status will not likely be attained. Consequently, the attack of some liberal arts people, in which they denied the premise that teaching is a profession, merely served to strengthen the hands of the National Education Association, regional and state associations of public school teachers, and other similar organizations in the determination of teachers to gain professional stature. To the profound disappointment of teachers, again they were experiencing not merely no assistance but criticisms from liberal arts professors, as the public school teachers and teacher education people were endeavoring to attain what to them was a laudable ambition—the achievement of professional status and sound academic improvement.

A second contention shared by many liberal arts people was that the extension of professional accrediting into this area of teacher education was completely unnecessary, since it could be adequately served by the regional associations. [Author's note: there are six regional accrediting agencies which accredit colleges and universities—and often secondary schools—on their total programs.] This argument fails to take into account the fact that all professions, as early as medieval times, have sought to control the preparation for and admission to their ranks. . . . Here again teacher education has initiated no new departure but has merely followed the examples of its peers, in which the professions (such as medicine) are not willing to rely on the lists of regionally accredited institutions for approval of professional programs of study. What is more, there is not likely to be any change in this attitude among the well-recognized professions.

. . .

This leads to the third and last major argument of the liberal arts people against NCATE. Their contention that NCATE as originally organized did not provide for a proper and appropriate balance of control was sound. Since the teacher education people had generally been anxious to have liberal arts participation in this new accrediting organization, there was comparatively little difficulty in reaching an agreement on a revised structure. The real difficulty was, and in fact still is, to find a constructive method whereby liberal arts individuals can be appointed to the Council. Several years ago, when NCATE was recognized by the National Commission on Accrediting, a temporary method for selecting liberal arts individuals was devised. Now we are in the process of finding an improved and more substantial procedure. Although all parties directly concerned are sincerely anxious to work together congenially and constructively, the solution to this problem is not easy.

The last eight words quoted above may be a masterpiece of understatement.

Selden pleaded for reconciliation of the two factions, a plea in perfect harmony with the theme of the TEPS conferences, and he added:

The influence of the liberal arts people will be negative if they incorrectly assume that teacher education has no place in the total education of teachers; or if they blatantly criticize schools of education for sometimes having been a haven for the less academically competent without recognizing that their own sometimes derogatory approach has often been a partial influence in encouraging this situation. In the same way, the influence of the teacher education people will be harmful if they over-emphasize the importance of teacher education courses and if they subordinate academic accomplishment and intellectual stimulation to such factors as social adjustment and playground supervision.

Chancellor Samuel B. Gould of the University of California, Santa Barbara, expressed the liberal arts view, as described by Selden above, when he declared in a major conference address at San Diego that there should be concentration on "the essence of accreditation instead of its peripheral elements."

To me the essence of accreditation is the examination of the teacher and the learning process. If I were to have my way (and I am sure that I shall not), I would strip away all else and go about the business of accreditation by the simple means of judging the quality of the teacher and the climate of the campus. I would try to get some notion of what is important on the campus and how that important something relates to the real reason for having an educational institution at all. I think I would learn more from sitting in the classroom than from sitting in conferences and committee meetings; from visiting groups of students in their residence halls and finding out what interests them than from poring over endless reports and charts and graphs; from eavesdropping on the conversations of the faculty or from talking with them about their teaching attitudes than from weighing the poundage of their research papers. I would not look for all things in all people, but rather for the way in which a group of individual faculty members can complement one another and by so doing create a community of intellectual interests.

This would be a radical approach and would make for a far more subjective judgment, immeasurable, intangible, and probably much less satisfying or conclusive. It would certainly be a less orderly approach. But a little disorder can sometimes exert a benign influence and certainly a democratic one. It is not nearly so important that students learn efficiently as that they learn the right things from the right people. . . .

It is difficult to quarrel with the views of Chancellor Gould, and certainly this particular layman is not going to try. The chancellor's idea of accreditation, however, does seem just a mite impractical. Counting the books in the library and adding up courses and hours may be a cumbersome, mechanical way to appraise an educational program, but it does have its practical aspects (which may be why the enumeration of library books, courses, and hours are considered essential in the accrediting of medical, dental, and law schools). I am left wondering where Chancellor Gould will find the people who are going to judge the quality of the teacher and the climate of the campus at 1,147 different teacher education institutions. If these people disagree on what makes up quality and how climate is to be defined, which seems at least likely, then the end result is not national standards but confusion bordering on chaos.

And a national standard of excellence—which is not to be confused with identical programs—would seem to be what teacher education in this country badly needs today.

CHAPTER SEVENTEEN

"Nobody Asked Me, But . . ."

If Sputnik I, bless it, did nothing else for this country, it multiplied many-fold our production of experts on education. Everybody knows what is wrong with our schools and our teachers and our children—particularly the neighbor's children. It is true, of course, that many of the people who know all the answers do not know all the questions, but this has its advantages, too—it makes for a spirited exchange of biases and prejudices. At the three TEPS conferences everyone was given a chance to say what teacher education ought to be in this country. In fact, a considerable part of the Kansas Conference was spent letting people say what they would do "If I Had My Way." The trouble is that these people were all experts of one sort or another, either professional educators or academic scholars, and little time was set aside for the inexperienced layman, such as a newspaperman whose knowledge of teacher education may be limited to what he reads in the paper—after he has written it. Let me take that time now and examine what seemed to be the most promising of all the ideas discussed at Bowling Green, Kansas, and San Diego.

I would start off by first seeing to it that all "good" teachers were paid a minimum of $12,000 a year. I am not sure just what I mean by "good," but I should think it would mean someone who had the equivalent of a master's degree, five or six years of classroom experience, and a dedication to teaching as a full-time career. This is going to be expensive, particularly with such a loose definition, but I know of no other way to lure into the teaching profession the kind of student I want. It is quite likely that such a salary scale would reward many teachers who do not deserve such rewards, but my plan would have all undeserving teachers weeded out of the schools in a generation or so. My $12,000 minimum salary is going to attract so many excellent teacher candidates that there will be no openings for the less-than-excellent, and it will make it well worthwhile for them to tackle the rough and tough program of preparation I have in mind.

Next, I would set up a five-year undergraduate program, the equivalent of at least 150 semester hours of work (compared to the present four-year program of 120 semester hours). Every future teacher, whether aiming for elementary-school or high-school teaching, would be required to have a solid major, in the neighborhood of 60 semester hours. For the secondary-school teacher, this major would be in the subject which the student plans to teach; the elementary-school teacher would major in one of the humanities.

In addition, every teacher candidate would have a minimum of 40 semester hours of English, because every teacher is, to some extent, a teacher of English. I expect these teachers of mine to demand considerable written work from their students, no matter what courses they are teaching. It may be a bit difficult for an algebra teacher to assign very much in the way of written themes, but it should be done wherever possible.

Every prospective teacher also needs a thorough foundation in psychology, with emphasis on child growth and development. I suppose this ought to total 9 to 12 semester hours. He also needs about 6 hours in the history and philosophy of education. As a matter of fact, I would require both of these courses of all college students. Nearly all students will become parents eventually and will need to know something about child psychology, and certainly every adult American needs to have an understanding of the history and philosophy of education, whether as a parent, a taxpayer, or just as a citizen. Education is too important to be ignored by any segment of our population.

Thus far we have used up about 115 of our 150 semester hours, although those students majoring in English would have another 40 free hours. (I will get to them in a moment.) Those who have concentrated in the sciences should use much of their remaining time studying the humanities, and those who have concentrated in the humanities should do some studying of science. Any time left over should be used for courses they want to take just for the fun of it.

I would encourage—almost to the point of insistence—every prospective teacher majoring in English to take 40 hours in *one* foreign language. Thus, all future foreign language teachers would have 60 hours of the language and 40 hours of English, and all future English teachers would have 60 hours of English and 40 hours of a second language. The teaching of both English and the foreign language would be vastly improved.

Throughout this five-year program, the students would be "exposed" to children of different ages. It might be on the playground, in youth clubs, or in the classroom. During this period they could decide with which age level they want to work after they have their certificates—and they may decide, too, that they do not really like children and ought to get into another field.

At the end of the five years, my student would be given a special degree. I am not sure what the degree should be called; it ought to carry more weight than just a Bachelor of Arts; it cannot be Bachelor of Arts in Teaching because such degree holders would inevitably be called "Old BATs"; and it cannot be Master of Arts in Teaching, because they are not masters of teaching yet.

During the summer between the awarding of this degree and the starting of the school year in the fall, the prospective teachers would spend nine weeks in summer school. Here they would get short but concentrated courses in such things as the use of audio-visual aids, tests and measurements, and materials. This also would be a good time for them to get an introduction to the various methods of teaching they will need to know.

Come fall, my students begin a year of internship. This does not mean sending them out to just any old school to do their student teaching. They are sent to carefully selected schools to work under the supervision of specially trained teachers. The supervising teacher is all-important here; I do not want my students picking up bad habits from bad teachers. During their fourth or fifth year in college, their "exposure" to children has been in the classroom, at the grade level at which they expect to teach. After maybe six weeks of working with the supervising teacher in the classroom, they take responsibility for the class for the remainder of the school year—but always with the help and guidance of the supervisor. Because the students are taking over the classroom, they should be on salary. I should think $4,000 would be about right.

Naturally, we have been weeding out the incompetents as we go along. No grade below a "B minus" would be accepted for any course in the student's major, and no grade below a "C" would be accepted for anything. Those who are not mentally, physically, or emotionally equipped for the classroom would be eased from the program. The year of internship is the last major check point. If the student shows that he just does not qualify as a teacher, he is denied a recommendation for a license, and what my teacher education institution recommends is the final word with the state certification authorities. This may be harsh treatment for a young man or woman who has spent six years preparing for a career, but the welfare of the children he would be teaching is far more important than the career of any individual. In any event, it is not likely that the incompetents are going to survive the first five years of the program.

At the end of the internship, the student teacher and his supervisor know his strengths and weaknesses, so we bring him back to college for a year of graduate work. It may be that the secondary-school teacher wants or needs more depth in his subject of specialization. Perhaps the elementary-school teacher finds that he is weaker than he supposed in history or in geography, or feels he needs more psychology. Perhaps our student teacher finds he has an aptitude for teaching remedial reading, or for working with retarded children, or for teaching gifted students in accelerated classes. Whatever he needs to give him the finishing touches as a really "good" teacher, we give him. I am not concerned with whether these graduate courses are in the graduate or undergraduate school; I want to be sure only that he is getting the courses he needs. In the same way, I am not concerned with whether the courses throughout his preparation have been given by the professional educators or the scholars, in the school of education or the college of liberal arts. I want to be sure only that he gets the best possible teachers and the best possible courses.

Now, indeed, is our teacher ready for an advanced degree, such as Master of Arts in Teaching. Perhaps we could stretch a point and call him a Master of the Fine Art of Teaching. When he embarks on his career as a full-fledged teacher he should receive a salary of about $7,000 a year. Satisfactory performance in the classroom (and by this I mean more than just ordinary competence because he is a really superior teacher) should bring him up to $10,000 to $12,000 within five or six years. After that his salary increases would depend upon continued study. (At that salary level he should be able to devote several summers to further study in depth in his field.) Wherever he teaches, he should be able to look forward to qualifying eventually for a salary of at least $14,000—twice his starting scale.

The teacher my proposed system would produce would be granted a certificate by the state education department, and I would expect that certificate to be recognized as valid in any state of the union. It might carry an endorsement setting forth the grade level for which he was prepared, or the subject matter which he was qualified to teach, but such endorsement would be primarily for information purposes. My teacher would be so much in demand that he would never have to bow to "requests" that he teach outside his field of specialization. If this be treason to the too-small high schools which must demand that its teachers tackle several unrelated subjects, so be it; they will just have to combine with their neighboring too-small high schools into one big-enough school which can guarantee every pupil the education he has a right to expect.

Under this plan I would expect the teacher shortage to be eliminated in fairly short order. The monetary rewards, and the status, that my teacher would receive would lure hundreds of thousands of our very best students into the teaching profession, and, as these superior teachers took over the classrooms, the incompetents and the part-timers would be forced out. The competent, but only ordinary, teachers would be forced to raise their own standards or look for other jobs.

Did someone say that young men and women cannot afford to spend seven years preparing for a teaching career? Well, dentists and lawyers spend that many years in preparation, and doctors spend much longer. To get the type of salaries that true professionals deserve, our teachers must have truly professional training. And if they become true professionals, I think the American people will be glad to pay them what they deserve.

PART II

By T. M. Stinnett

CHAPTER EIGHTEEN

Healing the Schisms in Education

The chief task of education in the future is to upgrade drastically the intellectual and technical competence of our teachers. This is surely a truism, because obviously this is where we must begin in any attempt to lift the quality of education. One of the real keys to this difficult task lies in the attitudes of those in higher education who are involved in the preparation of teachers. This demands a constant search for the means of healing the existing schisms in education at all levels, but especially in higher education.

If these efforts are to succeed beyond some surface gains, there are some tough, irritating factors to be faced. C. P. Snow, in the 1959 Rede Lecture at Cambridge, discusses the disturbing schism between the literary intellectuals and the scientists. There is here an analogy, perhaps a diluted one, to the infighting which obtains in the United States between the so-called scholars and the so-called educationists. Having spent most of his life in research in physics, but at the same time being engaged in extensive writing, this distinguished Englishman became well acquainted with the representatives of both cultures.

There have been plenty of days when I have spent the working hours with scientists and then gone off at night with some literary colleagues. . . . It was through living among these groups . . . that I felt I was moving among two groups—comparable in intelligence, identical in race, not grossly different in social origin, earning about the same incomes, who had almost ceased to communicate at all, who in intellectual, moral, and psychological climate had so little in common that instead of going from Burlington House or South Kensington to Chelsea, one might have crossed the ocean. . . . By and large this is a problem of the entire West.

. . . . .

I believe the intellectual life of the whole Western society is increasingly being split into two polar groups. . . . At one pole we have the literary intellectuals—at the other, scientists. Between the two, a gulf of mutual incomprehension [exists]. They have a curious distorted image of each other. Their attitudes are so different that, even on the level of emotion, they can't find much common ground.[1]

What is the nature of the analogy for teacher education? Every professional discipline has had a long and bitter fight to gain a respected place in higher education—here and elsewhere. English did. Science did. Teacher education as a professional process, as did science, had to get its start in separate institutions. But now, to the distress of some, it is moving into the mainstream of higher education. This argues eloquently for bridging the gap of cultures in higher education.

The recent observation of a college president is germane to the point.

On this campus, the scientists deplore their paucity of knowledge of the humanities and wish they could learn more. The humanists boast that they know nothing about science and assert loudly that they have no desire to acquire any knowledge in the field.

How accurate or significant this is, we do not know. We could assume, first, that the college president is a scientist. Second, we could assume that on another campus the same attitudes might be found, but reversed.

The American people need to bring to bear upon the current educational scene the perspective of history and wise divination. In recent years we have been engaging in educational controversy without restraint, as if the goal were the complete obliteration of one side or the other. One may question whether we are carefully mindful of our past and whether we are misreading our future.

Actually, the controversy in education, especially that about teacher education, goes much deeper than the struggle of rival wills, much deeper than the clamor for predominance by one set of educational power patterns, much deeper than a struggle between two personality clusters or two philosophical camps, although all of these are involved to some degree. The struggle, rather, is the result of the coalescence of several factors. One is the sudden acceleration of the tempo of life under the impact of recent and staggering achievements in science. Another is the shift in the balance of knowledge. Still another is the rather sudden shift in the power sources of nations. The new power source—and only yesterday it was colonialism or sea power or air power—is intellectual power. The resulting intellectual revolution has catapulted science into the lexicon of the liberally educated man.

[1] C. P. Snow, *The Two Cultures and the Scientific Revolution,* The Rede Lecture, 1959 (New York: Cambridge University Press, 1959), pp. 2-4.

Too, the impinging of the population explosion upon the non-renewable resources compels man to husband reverently the bounties of nature and to create from the frontiers of his own mind additional means of subsistence. Such drastic shifts in the nature of things inevitably strip the veneer of custom and tradition from current practices and markedly expose dangerous obsolescences.

These new factors, one surmises, largely explain the present tumult and shouting in education. Something of the same sort of thing happened to us militarily in 1941. The answer we found then is the answer we must find now—the constructive and rapid eradication of the obsolescences, the updating of processes geared to the demands of new and revolutionary forces, and not an obsession with finding the guilty culprits. But this is difficult for a society to do. Scapegoating and self-righteousness are most appealing postures for the egos of men. Thus, there is widespread superficiality in the reading of the times. There are breast-beating lamentations about the spreading disease of conformity, which we lay at the door of the wrong kind of education, to the point that some have made non-conformity a new religion of conformity. Actually, what is tending to permeate our society is not so much the virus of conformity as the inevitable price exacted by fragmentation and extreme specialization, which tend not only to eliminate the whole man but to make him unmindful of the real meaning of our common life.

Under the impact of these frustrating forces, many of our intellectuals are exhibiting the willfulness of children who, failing to inculcate their own standards by edict, indulge in the ego-satisfying act of repudiating the society in which they have their being. They wash their hands of the hard, slow task of elevation. So we are witnessing a national crying jag of self-pity. It is next to impossible to get anything published today that is not condemning something. The cult of the negativists has become a new dispensation, to which only those who deny, in haughty verbalism, the power of affirmation are admitted. The members of this cult, in their splendid isolation, cry out bitterly at a Jerusalem that refuses to be saved—on their own terms.

This is a new thing under the sun in America—this self-depreciation. A century ago the youthful and perceptive Alexis de Tocqueville wrote of an America "where no boundary seems to be fixed to men's efforts"; and of the American as one who "in his eyes, [believes that] what he has not yet done is only that which he has not yet attempted to do." If Americans now listen to and read the vocal critics—those who by virtue of their privileged position in education, in the literary world, and in the arts ought to be leading and seeking constructive ways out of our dilemma—they will find themselves inundated with the theses of despair and defeat. They will find themselves pictured as stolid, cud-chewing cattle, incapable of serious thought, insensitive to any higher virtues than soap operas, beer, and gadgetry, with no larger dreams, with no divine aspirations, nothing except preoccupation with full bellies, licentiousness, and mobocracy.

Thomas Griffith has paid his respects to this strange effort to downgrade America.

I have sometimes wished that a newspaper might preface its coverage in this way:

"The news we bring you today is a melancholy collection—murders, frauds and accidents, bickering between politicians who exaggerate our differences, racial tensions that dishonor the Christianity we profess, failures in productivity, and quarrels among allies. From the half of the world that is Communist, we are able to bring you only their boasts of strength. We do not know what fights are going on there that might be far more deadly than any disagreement among our allies. We print a photograph of one Negro cuffed to the ground in Alabama, but we do not know how many people were herded off to 'voluntary' labor in Tientsin last night. While our reporters bunched themselves around a German courtroom to see one G.I. tried, we do not know what miscarriage of justice went unmarked in Bokhara or what betrayal of the human spirit took place in Smolensk. If we could bring you the rest of today's news, we might not think less of our own failings, but at least we would not think them unique, and we might find tyranny more evil than we knew and less sure of itself than we thought. So forgive us our omissions, but keep them in mind, for we have done only half our job." [2]

One wonders how fruitful in the long look is the present fetish of viewing Americans as pygmies and the Russians as ten feet tall. One wonders if any really constructive purpose is served by the current drive to stereotype the so-called common man and some educators as ignorant louts, as the very antithesis of their critics in terms of intellectual status and virtue as well. Self-flagellation as a catharsis is one thing; as an inducer of abject depreciation, it is quite another.

The proper education of Americans is of the greatest significance and we must take a hard look, because in essence it is a look at what education in America is now and what it must be like in the years we are coming to. For however good the procedures in education which predominated yesterday, that was yesterday; but today and the todays of the future bring new tasks and therefore some new imperatives. Here are set forth some of the musts, as we grope for ways to step up the quality of education.

[2] Thomas Griffith, *The Waist-High Culture* (New York: Harper & Brothers, 1959), pp. 136-37.

The quality and the effectiveness of teacher education, in a large measure, depend upon the extent to which it becomes a prime concern of the whole institution and of every type of first-class institution in American life.

Parochialism, both as to staff and institutions, regarding this fundamental field of responsibility must end.

To examine the role of the institution first: The unfortunate but necessary separateness of teacher education as a professional process from the mainstream of higher education, which has obtained in America until recent years, is ending. Some seventy-five single-purpose teacher education institutions (teachers colleges) have disappeared in this country since 1951—about thirty-five in the last three years. There are now only seventy-three public and twelve private ones left. The single-purpose teacher education institution in American life is disappearing; it is becoming the general-purpose state college and has, to a large extent, already evolved into the state university.

There is no good point in belaboring the reasons for this separateness which has existed all these years. The point is that it is ending and, at long last, teacher education is beginning to take its rightful place alongside the other professional disciplines in higher education.

It is not historically true to say that in America teacher education, as a professional process, withdrew from the liberal arts. It never was there. It is just now fighting its way to be there. It belongs there. And it is not unfair to assert that many prestige institutions in this country, while originally established to prepare ministers and teachers, defaulted somewhere along the way in pursuit of more prestigious occupations for their graduates.

The reasons and motives involved in this default are diverse and complex, and there is no good point in reviving them. But this is clear now: if the prestige institutions, if the liberal arts institutions, expect to affect materially the quality of education in this country through the curriculum and the caliber of teaching, then there is only one realistic, effective way they can do it. They must get into teacher education in a serious and not a token manner. They must assume responsibility for improvement. They must shed the role of elder statesmen who, from the sidelines, indulge in Monday morning quarterbacking. Pontifical pronouncements delivered from the safe haven of isolation can never be as effective as judgments from the battlefield.

In addition to the need for the involvement of prestige institutions in teacher education is the need for sympathetic concern by their total staffs.

We speak glibly of the schism between liberal arts and education professors. A more serious schism, however, is that which exists between the liberal arts professor and his counterpart in the elementary and secondary schools in the persistent refusal of the former to become involved as a resource person for the latter in the overhauling of the curriculum and the lifting of the quality of teaching in the lower schools. As long as this disengagement exists, the schools will never be what the prestige colleges or their teachers would like them to be.

Many believe that this idea of involvement of liberal arts professors in the prosaic problems of the schools is an idle dream. The president of the State University of Iowa, in a speech before the annual session of the American Council on Education, said:

When in the 1870's and '80's and '90's the learned doctors and professors of our universities and colleges felt it beneath their dignity to prepare teachers for the common schools, the need was met by the proliferation of normal schools and teachers colleges throughout the land. Nor should we expect the current need to be met by a transitory interest of the learned doctors and professors. It would be a glorious prospect if they could be expected to concern themselves in a long-range program for the improvement of schools. But they will not. Neither their professional interest nor their professional advancement by the criteria which they, themselves, have set lie in that quarter. Within five years most, if not all, the present critics among them will have returned to *Beowulf* or Chaucer or the political policies of Sir Robert Walpole or the causes of the French Revolution, or the peaceful uses of atomic power; and high-school teachers of English and social studies and science will again find it necessary to turn to the professional educationists who are their only constant and true friends in time of need.[3]

In a recent conference on teacher education, the great need for the liberal arts professor to become a resource person for teachers in the elementary and secondary schools was discussed. The dean of a liberal arts college said:

I wish this were possible, but I don't think it is. You see, it is a matter of prestige and status. The head of one of our science departments, a highly competent scientist, has made the improvement of teaching in his field in the elementary and secondary schools a matter of first priority. He has worked diligently for years with public-school teachers in conferences in our state workshops, and in preservice and inservice credit courses. There is no question that he has had profound influence in lifting the level of the curriculum and of the teaching in our schools. But he is low man on the totem pole in his own department. Why? Quite naturally, the time he might have spent in research and writing—and he's extremely able in both as revealed in the

[3] Virgil M. Hancher, "The Challenges We Face," *The Educational Record* 40: 12-13; January 1959.

work of his early years—has gone into these efforts to upgrade courses and teaching in the public schools. As a result, he is not highly regarded by his colleagues because he has not produced the research or the publications which might have earned their respect.

There is another new and promising side to this coin. Many of the scholarly societies have, in recent years, voluntarily and vigorously joined in the task of improving the curriculum and teaching in the public schools. Among these scholarly groups are the American Council of Learned Societies, the American Association for the Advancement of Science, the National Academy of Sciences-National Research Council, the Modern Language Association of America, the National Council of Teachers of English, the American Historical Association, the American Institute of Biological Sciences, and many others. This involvement appears to be one of the most significant things currently happening in education. Its significance, in great part, lies in the fact that the scholars themselves are more sensitive to the interests of their professional associations than to any other influence.

The extent to which teacher education is becoming a matter of concern of the total institution is reflected in a survey made by the Council on Cooperation in Teacher Education during the summer of 1960. A total of 1,074 senior colleges and universities approved for teacher education in 1959-60 were polled on the question: "Does your institution have a committee or council on teacher education?" Table 18-1 reflects the nature of the replies.

Almost one-half (360) of the responding institutions (768) indicated that they had established such a cooperative body. When those responding "No, but . . ." are taken into account, perhaps as many as two-thirds of the responding institutions have set up all-institution committees of some kind on teacher education. Another significant aspect of the CCTE survey is that 87 per cent of these committees have been established since 1950, and 40 per cent of the total were established between 1958 and 1960, concurrent with the three cooperative conferences described herein.

The professional unit for teacher education in colleges and universities will continue, and the same kind of autonomy will obtain for it as is true of the other professional units.

This fact of life must be faced up to by all segments of higher education. It is easy to sense vague hopes on the part of some that a partnership in the preparation of teachers means the elimination or emasculation of the professional aspects of the preparation of teachers. This seems to be a total misreading of all the signs. The difference will be in the cooperative planning of these programs and

TABLE 18-1

PREVALENCE OF CAMPUS-WIDE COMMITTEES OR COUNCILS FOR TEACHER EDUCATION, JUNE 1960

	Total Questionnaires Mailed		Total Replies		Negative Responses		Negative "But" Responses		Affirmative Responses	
	No.	% of Total	No.	% of Total Sent	No.	% of Total Ret.	No.	% of Total Ret.	No.	% of Total Ret.
Liberal Arts Colleges	551	51.3	386	70.1	153	39.6	69	17.9	164	42.5
Teachers Colleges	99	9.2	66	66.7	14	21.2	22	33.3	30	
Multipurpose { Public Univ.	93	8.6	73	78.5	21	28.8	15	20.5	37	
Private	128	11.9	99	77.3	23	23.2	18	18.2	58	
State Coll.	154	14.3	119	77.2	26	21.8	24	20.2	69	
Miscellaneous (Incl. Technical Schools)	49	4.6	25	51.0	18	72.0	5	20.0	2	8.0
	Total 1074	% 99.9	Total 786	% 71.5	Total 255	% 33.3	Total 153	% 19.9	Total 360	% 46.9

SOURCE: Council on Cooperation in Teacher Education, American Council on Education

policies and a resultant improvement of the professional and academic offerings. The professionals, likewise, should not deceive themselves with the notion that changes are not going to be made in the programs of schools and departments of education. The chances are great that these needed changes will both strengthen teacher education and increase the status of the professional unit. There are weaknesses in the present structure, yes; however, the answer lies not in the abolition of these units but in the amelioration of what has been termed, with some validity, the monolithic nature of their control of teacher education.

What is the basis for the belief that the professional unit will be strengthened and continued? Because the history of development of all professions points up the necessity for responsible units exercising unilateral control for recruitment, selection, guidance, retention, placement, coordination, inservice growth, and many other factors. Without such a unit, these responsibilities become nobody's business. If we are to assume that teaching is not and cannot be a profession, if we are to assume that teaching has nothing that is unique in terms of skills and knowledge and techniques—a uniqueness which distinguishes all other professions—then this thesis is invalid.

Former Chancellor Kimpton of the University of Chicago has written:

Finally, let us explore the proper relationships of the schools of education to the departments of our colleges and universities. If the schools of education have a kind of monopolistic hold upon the high-school curriculum and the training of secondary-school teachers, it is only because no one else has paid any attention to them. The schools of education are going to continue this control; hence the problem is how to focus all of the resources of higher education upon these problems in the schools of education.[4]

And he added this significant sentence: "Wastelands have been known to produce excellent crops, given effort and ingenuity."

Never has the climate been more favorable for a real partnership among all elements in higher education and practitioners in our public schools regarding teacher education.

Somehow, there has to be developed some kind of brake upon the continued proliferation and fragmentation of college courses.

There are repeated and bitter charges about the proliferation of education courses, and many of these are justified. But the same criticisms can be directed at all of higher education.

Shortly after World War II, Ernest Hocking, then professor at Harvard, taught for a time in a Dutch university and was impressed

---

[4] Lawrence A. Kimpton, "Remarks of the Retiring Chairman," *The Educational Record* 40:35; January 1959.

with the small number of courses offered there. Upon his return to Harvard he counted something like 1,200 courses in the Harvard catalog. He summed it up somewhat in this way:

> What of the capacity of the student? Does that also increase by large multiples as the years pass? Two hundred years ago his capacity was about 16 courses in four years. Today it is still about 16 courses. If 200 years ago he had 64 courses to choose from, he could absorb a quarter of what he was offered. When the offering reached 640 courses, he could absorb a fortieth. With 1,280 courses, he can absorb perhaps an eightieth of the whole.[5]

Now this sin or evil, if it is a sin or evil, is a very natural thing. This proliferation is not built upon the needs of students. It is built upon the intellectual interests of the professors, and it is not confined to schools of education. A distinguished biologist recently commented that the trouble with his field was fragmentation. He named one American university that offers twenty-six separate introductory courses in biology.

Major adjustments in the teacher education programs and in certification are indicated.

One is flexibility in the preparation programs. The faculty of the School of Education at the University of Wisconsin has approved and put into operation the use of proficiency examinations. This policy provides that the student must complete the bachelor's degree, including student teaching. But in any other course in the teaching field, or any professional course, the student may demonstrate competence through a proficiency examination. This is the kind of flexibility we need in professional education. One of the things that puts professional education in an untenable position is the insistence that every student must run sheeplike through exactly the same sequence of courses. This does not make much sense to anybody.

A second area of needed adjustment is that of flexibility in certification prescriptions, by which some liberal arts graduates can secure initial certification and by which experienced teachers can secure authorization to teach in other fields without having to run the whole gamut of piling up credits in every prescribed course. In all probability, we shall see a growing use of proficiency examinations. The state of West Virginia in 1958 instituted an examination for liberal arts graduates. Of the 119 who took the examination in October, more than half failed it.

[5] B. Othanel Smith, "A Joint Task: the Preparation of a Teacher," *Journal of Teacher Education* 10: 191; June 1959.

Such a proposal, quite naturally, is disturbing to those who hold that teaching has reached fully recognized professional status. So this idea is equated with that of proposing short cuts that doctors may take into medical practice.

The assumption is made that the use of proficiency examinations means ultimately the abolition of professional preparation of teachers. This does not follow at all. This proposal simply points a way by which adjustment can be made for the bright youngster who has had interrelated courses but not the specific courses; who has had compensating and related experiences and who could demonstrate mastery of a given course in another way. There will be little of the skipping of prescribed programs and prescribed curriculums. After all, we are certificating 90,000 of these people (and others not so well qualified) every year on emergency certificates; and, in doing this, there is bound to be a concession of some degree of competence or this practice could not be defended. If a person has some degree of competence, why not use some technique that would permit him to demonstrate a portion of it? The proficiency examination is the lesser of two expediences, if the proficiency examination is an expedient.

There must be found a new, more realistic rationale for the process of certification, in addition to more effective procedures. These comments are not intended as a criticism of the state certification authorities. While there are exceptions, of course, in the main these authorities have tried to administer certification on the principle of the consent of the governed. The quarrel is with the teaching profession itself on the grounds that (1) it has not assumed in full measure its rightful obligation in connection with certification prescriptions; (2) its members have been vocal only to complain; and (3) its members have been too willing to resort to the easy procedure of using legal prescriptions to enforce indefensible requirements upon others.

As a result, the profession itself has tended to pressure the proliferation of requirements and certificates to the point of absurdity, to the point that each separate teaching field has been made into a sort of priesthood and the person who deviates by one course finds it difficult to get into the clan. We have pushed this trend so far that two states issue more than sixty separate certificates.

This has had its adverse influence upon the profession by proliferating it from one into many professions. The cure for this situation is, in the opinion of many, to restrict legal certification to certifying that the holder is a qualified teacher—in other words, that he has been selected, screened, and prepared; that he is a graduate of a high-quality institution and recommended by it—and this is as far as certification should be concerned. Competency for specialized assignments should be defined and certificated by professional organizations, as is the case with most other respected professions, and accreditation plus observance by every teacher of the accepted code of professional ethics should enforce appropriate teaching assignments.

Finally, the one sure means of improving the quality of teacher education is to institute, universally, highly selective procedures for admission into teacher education. No amount of tinkering with the curriculum or reshuffling of courses here and there will produce the improvements we must have, although these may be helpful. The indispensable need is to increase the intellectual caliber of those who prepare for teaching. Graduate students in education and a great many experienced teachers, as a general rule, do not question the quality of education courses or the teaching of them so much as they do the caliber of the people who pursue these courses.

This raises a related problem, the seriousness of which can be scarcely exaggerated. This is the all-too-prevalent attitude of liberal arts professors toward education courses. This attitude is vehemently antagonistic. The answer to the teacher shortage rests just here. Little faith can be placed in the repeated claims of some infinite and mythical pool of broadly educated people—housewives and others— who would come into teaching if only certification requirements were abolished. This is an illusory proposal for solving our teacher shortage. Liberal arts professors, in particular, have repeated this shibboleth until they seriously believe it to be true. Yet we have come upon times of great shortage of college teachers who do not have to meet certification requirements. Thus, the abolition of such requirements in the belief that this will solve the teacher shortage is illusory, to say the least. But there is a relatively untapped and relatively large pool of liberal arts students who scarcely ever hear anything good about teaching as a dignified career. If they hear anything at all about teaching from their liberal arts professors, it is likely to be a scathing denunciation of professional preparation. One may talk to hundreds of them and they will repeat all the old stereotypes about professional education. When they are asked what education courses they have pursued, almost without exception, the reply is that they have not been in any such courses at all. They have simply heard their liberal arts professors denounce the courses.

The downgrading of the professional preparation of teachers in recent years in the United States seems incredible in the light of history and in view of similar practices in other countries so admired by the critics; yet, some of the motivating factors are easily understood. The professors of education too often have justified their procedures upon slogans, clichés, and catchwords and too little upon validated research and scientific principles. They have sometimes been too casual in their own standards of scholarship and that of their intellectual offspring. They have frequently been arrogant toward their colleagues in higher education. They have often tended to welcome the default by the liberal arts professors of any responsibility for the preparation of teachers. Indeed, there occasionally has been the subtle use of the elbow technique to encourage such defaults. They have tended all too often to depreciate this regrettable default by attributing ignorance of teaching know-how to those who provide up to 80 per cent of the courses in teacher education. And perhaps they have claimed too much too often for their discipline.

This is one side of the coin. On the other, we quote a physics professor at Stanford:

On every campus of every large university there is a school, or perhaps a department, of education. The scientists hear that it is there, but they do not visit it very often. They are trying to teach the young and are realizing that the job is too hard for them. But while they go on with feelings of partial success, there is, nearby, this company of specialists in the philosophy and technique of the teaching process, and they make no use of them. . . .

I cannot dismiss this odd boycott . . . by declaring that 90 per cent of the educationists are fools led by the 10 per cent who are smart rogues. I know some educationists who seem to be as intelligent as physicists and as honest as mathematicians. They do not take pride in producing highly trained but ignorant teachers. They worry about some of the same educational problems that bother the scientists, but, with a better background in these areas, they worry more constructively. . . . But unless their whole discipline is fraudulent—and I do not believe it is—the rest of us do harm to our own disciplines . . . by pretending that they do not exist. I think that, sooner or later, teachers of all sorts are going to have to agree that there is some kind of scientific basis possible for what they are trying to do.

Whether or not the educationists know the answers, they are concerned with important questions. What is the real nature of the process of learning? How can one train the mind? Can people be taught to think, and if so how is it done? . . . Everyone who teaches needs the answers, even the man who is a "born teacher," whatever that phrase means. . . .

This argument cannot be dismissed by the ancient slogan of the anti-educationists, "All a teacher needs is to know his stuff." People who talk this way are logically as vulnerable as their opponents in the opposite corner who say, or have been said to say, "All a teacher needs is to know how to teach." . . . We are not going to find out what the right things are by shallow, empirical deductions. We need basic theory, and should at least sympathize with honest people who are trying to develop it. . . .[6]

[6] Paul Kirkpatrick, "On Colleagues and Clients," *Journal of Higher Education* 31: 413-14; November 1960.

What is the answer to this problem? That there are grounds for much criticism of education courses is obvious, but the continuing antagonism of the liberal arts people is not constructive. Perhaps both the improvement of education courses and the discontinuance of this kind of criticism on the part of the liberal arts professor must come along together. But both of these must come to pass, or the teacher shortage will not be solved.

Every sign one can read points to the need for a fresh look at the scope, purposes, and processes of American education. Obviously, we now have an age in education that is ending. The explosive nature of world conditions, in which the bitter dichotomies of the rich and the poor, of the well-fed and the hungry, of the industrialized and the primitive, can only lead to unimaginable tragedy unless the Western world moves—and moves in time—to eradicate these divisions; and the healing of schisms in education is fundamental to the search for the needed quality in education.

A fresh look at education has to be all-inclusive, including a reappraisal of processes, purposes, and patterns. We have made a beginning with all three. We are beginning to pull together the loose threads of our emphasis upon generalized education and are moving toward greater emphasis upon specialization.

But should we go all the way in emulation of the English system, with which many thoughtful Englishmen are disenchanted? We have made a beginning toward more rigor in the process. Should we go all the way in emulation of the Russians, who are beginning to pull back from the resulting excesses? A good guess is that we will make our educational adjustments to the scientific revolution by the democratic process of controversy and the balancing of proposed extremes. We must, therefore, cease being irritated with the sweeping criticisms of education, although many may seem unfair and may seem to ignore our history and dismiss our kind of society. We must also cease to be indignant at proposed radical reforms, although many may seem to be superficial, if not downright silly, because these are all parts of the decision-making processes of the American people.

Will we have the time for the processes to come to fruition? Can we, in fact rather than appearance, heal the schisms in the education of our teachers so that there is total commitment of institutions and staff to this indispensable approach to the achievement of the needed quality in education?

To quote C. P. Snow again:

Closing the gap between our cultures is a necessity in the most abstract intellectual sense, as well as in the most practical. When these two senses have grown apart, then no society is going to be able to think with wisdom.

For the sake of the intellectual life, for the sake of this country's special danger, for the sake of the Western society living precariously rich among the poor, for the sake of the poor who needn't be poor if there is intelligence in the world, it is obligatory for us and the Americans and the whole West to look at our education with fresh eyes. . . .

Isn't it time we began? The danger is, we have been brought up to think as though we have all the time in the world. We have very little time. So little that I dare not guess at it.[7]

[7] C. P. Snow, *op. cit.*, pp. 53-54.

CHAPTER NINETEEN

Who Prepares Our Teachers—and How?

A Summary of Current Practices

Some curious images of teachers in our elementary and secondary schools, of their preparation, and of their licensure have been implanted in the public mind.

The erroneous notion that the "dismal teachers colleges" are the prime or exclusive source of their preparation has been carefully, if unwittingly, nurtured. The notion that their preparation consists predominantly or entirely of methods courses has been stressed by the use of isolated cases. The notion that state teacher certification requirements consist exclusively of education courses and are fixed by an unholy conspiracy between professors of education and state boards of education has found expression in our newspapers and popular magazines. These stereotypes have had a serious impact upon the public's concept of teachers and teaching.

What are the facts?

Well, the facts are not all good. But they are not all bad either, not nearly so bad as the public and many educators have been led to believe. Extreme examples to sustain almost any preconceived viewpoint can be found in our system of mass education, if one searches long enough for them. In short, the situation is neither as good nor as bad as the pros or the cons would have it. But the undeniable fact remains that it is not as good as it ought to be. Great improvements are necessary all along the line, and the need for action is urgent.

In all fairness, one who attempts to assess the quality of American elementary and secondary schools must consider the history of those schools and the puzzling willingness of the American people to tolerate incredible conditions and weaknesses. Only a war or a sputnik seems to jar their complacency to the point of demanding the correction of dangerous lags.

An impartial observer will recognize that we have come a long way in a relatively short time, and the obvious fact is that when the present is placed alongside the past, these schools and the teaching profession have made remarkable progress in the face of great handicaps. For example, at the turn of the century the idea that anyone could teach was prevalent. For the elementary schools it was thought that the teacher needed to know only a little more than the little children. Of course, this concept was the product of our predominately rural society, where schools were small and the curriculum consisted of the rudiments of reading, writing, and ciphering and where "lickin' and larnin' " were synonymous. Teaching jobs in many communities (if not most) were regarded as sinecures for spinsters, indigents, and disabled soldiers; in short, members of the community whom somebody had to support otherwise.

Actually, these concepts still were dominant up to World War II. For example, as late as 1940 only nine states required beginning elementary-school teachers to have completed four years of college preparation. This number of states had grown to only seventeen by the beginning of the hectic decade of the 1950's. For the remainder of the states a beginning elementary-school teacher could be certified on preparation ranging from less than high-school graduation to three years of college.

Contrast this with the facts for 1961: forty-three states now enforce the minimum preparation of four years of college for beginning elementary-school teachers, and all states for beginning high-school teachers. (Of course, the teacher shortage compels many states to issue some emergency certificates, but forty-three states are enforcing this basic requirement for regular certification.) In anybody's book this is a remarkable advance in standards, even though the content and the quality of preparation are attacked vigorously by the critics. The fact remains that the professional preparation of teachers and state certification requirements have upgraded preparation requirements drastically, and, despite what the critics contend, the upgrading in the quantity of required subject-matter preparation has been the most pronounced. It certainly should not be contended that the content portion of teacher education is what it ought to be, in view of the vast accumulations of new knowledge and of new demands upon education. But when the average preparation of teachers in terms of college years has been stepped up from one year to nearly four in a little more than a decade, and when the average preparation of high-school teachers approaches the master's degree level, it cannot be fairly said that the subject-matter preparation has not been given serious attention. One has to look at where we were only a short time ago to get a real perspective of where we are now.

Teachers College Whipping Boy

Who prepares our teachers? Are the teachers colleges the prime source? Are they the culprits? They would seem so, from what one reads.

This writer commented, in an editorial in the *Journal of Teacher Education,* on this strange myth[1] as follows:

Berating the teachers colleges has become a litany. It has become one of the remarkable phases of a rather sustained period of criticism of education and educationists. The lowly teachers college seems to have become a sort of whipping boy for every malcontent who has a pain about education but can't locate it exactly. It has been made into a sort of symbol of alleged academic inferiority. Worst of all, it has become a stereotype for the focus of vituperation. One wonders why and whether the critics aren't really belaboring a straw man.

One supposes that it all started with the caricaturing of teachers colleges in an article in *Life*'s special issue devoted to the schools (October 16, 1950, pp. 147-54). . . .

The article, "Who Teaches the Teacher?" by John William Sperry, who is—as everybody knows—the celebrated Sloan Wilson, was directed at the state teachers colleges. The title of the article implies, for the casual reader, that the faculties of these benighted institutions prepare all of the nation's teachers or a preponderance of them, although the author frankly admits he doesn't know the number but says a "big percentage" of the elementary- and secondary-school teachers in the United States. These institutions were then turning out each year little more than one in five of our teachers. But this article, as far as we can find, set off the caterwauling; and the yelping has steadily grown in volume since.

We would like to assume that really the critics are talking about all teacher education institutions (all 1,207 of them), including our finest state universities, many of our famed liberal arts colleges and prestige Ivy League institutions—but the language of many of the indictments does not seem to justify this assumption. If such an assumption were made, then we are smack up against the fact that from four-fifths to six-sevenths of the total degree program for the education of teachers is provided by the liberal arts or academic faculties of these institutions. Can we assume that the critics intend to call the Ivy League colleges, for example, all of which with one or two exceptions we find on the approved list of teacher education institutions, teachers colleges? We think not. We think they are talking about, as was the *Life* article, the state teachers colleges.

Since then, it has been the vogue to ascribe most of the supposed ills of

[1] T. M. Stinnett, "The Teachers College Myth," *Journal of Teacher Education* 7: 290, 366-68; December 1956.

teacher education, the blame for the teacher shortage, the alleged deterioration of education in general, to these "dismal institutions." Over and over these criticisms seem to be based upon the assumption that the teachers colleges are predominant in the preparation of teachers. There are references to "the teachers college monopoly," "the mandarins of the teachers colleges," "the stranglehold of the teachers colleges."

. . .

Consider *first* the number and designation of institutions preparing teachers. What kinds and how many colleges and universities are engaged in teacher education? . . . A quick check of the list of 1,207 institutions approved by the respective state school legal authorities for teacher education in 1955-56 . . . indicates that there were 107 teachers colleges and state colleges of education, as separate institutions on this list; 99 state general colleges; 92 state universities and land-grant colleges; 55 private universities; 23 municipal colleges and universities; 550 private liberal arts colleges; 129 technical and professional schools—a total of 1,055 institutions offering four years or more of college work. In addition, there were 152 approved junior colleges, making a grand total of 1,207 institutions authorized to prepare teachers in 1955-56.

Consider *second* the actual role of teachers colleges in the preparation of teachers. Some of the foregoing statements, as has been said, seem to imply that teachers colleges prepare all—or almost all—of our teachers. The fact is that, in 1954-55, the public and non-public teachers colleges prepared only 23 per cent of the elementary-school teachers, 18.4 per cent of the high-school teachers, and 20.4 per cent of the total completing preparation in that year.[2]

What institutions prepared the remainder?

The answer is the public and non-public general colleges and universities (not including the teachers colleges). The private liberal arts colleges and universities in 1954-55 prepared 30.1 per cent of the elementary-school teachers, 32.8 per cent of the high-school teachers, and 31.6 per cent of all teachers prepared that year. Public colleges and universities not including the teachers colleges prepared 56.9 per cent of the elementary-school teachers, 48.8 per cent of the high-school teachers, and 48.0 per cent of all teachers prepared that year.

Publicly controlled institutions of all types (including state teachers colleges) prepared 68.2 per cent of the elementary-school teachers, 65.2 per cent of the high-school teachers, and 66.5 per cent of all teachers in 1954-55; privately controlled institutions of all kinds prepared 31.8 per cent of all teachers in that year. The reader should bear in mind that the above figures refer to the annual production of new teachers, to the new teachers completing preparation in the stated years, and not to the total teaching staff.

[2] "The 1956 Teacher Supply and Demand Report," prepared by the NEA Research Division in cooperation with NCTEPS, *Journal of Teacher Education* 7: 44-45; March 1956.

Let's look at the situation in 1960. Who prepares our teachers? Table 19-1 reflects the institutional situation for the school year 1959-60.

TABLE 19-1

NUMBER AND TYPES OF TEACHER EDUCATION INSTITUTIONS
IN THE UNITED STATES, 1960

Types of Institutions	Public	Private	Total
Teachers Colleges	73	12	85
Universities	93	128	221
General and Liberal Arts Colleges	154	551	705
Technical Schools, Junior Colleges, and Unclassified			122
			1,133

SOURCE: T. M. Stinnett, "Certification Requirements and Procedures Among the States in 1960," *Journal of Teacher Education* 11:173-84; June 1960

What percentage of our newly prepared teachers—those who graduate from college each year—will have come from each of these types of institutions in 1961? We shall have to use the latest available data from the 1958 graduating classes; a total of 114,411 graduates had prepared for teaching. Of this number, 20 per cent came from the teachers colleges (23.7 per cent of the new elementary-school teachers and 17.6 per cent of the new high-school teachers). About 44 per cent came from the general or liberal arts colleges (43.3 per cent of the new elementary-school teachers and 45.1 per cent of the high-school teachers), with an almost equal division between the public and the private colleges. The universities produced 35.6 per cent (public universities, 25.3 per cent and private universities, 10.3 per cent). Public institutions of all types prepared about two-thirds and private institutions about one-third of the new teachers in this year.[3]

Thus, it is apparent that the blame for whatever ills afflict teacher education cannot be laid to the teachers colleges alone. All types of colleges and universities, public and private, good, bad, and indifferent institutions, and many of the great-name colleges and universities are involved.

[3] National Education Association, Research Division, *Teacher Supply and Demand in Public Schools, 1959,* Research Report 1959-R6 (Washington, D. C.: National Education Association, 1959), p. 14.

What About Teacher Certification?

Then there is the charge that the licensure requirements of the states overemphasize education courses and discount good solid content courses. What are the facts? In 1960 the median requirement of the states in professional courses for the degree certificate for elementary-school teachers was 24 semester hours out of the usual 120 to 124 required for a degree. This is one-fifth of the degree program, leaving four-fifths (96 semester hours) for work in the academic fields. The range among the states is from 16 to 36 semester hours in professional courses.

For high-school teachers, the median requirement in education courses is 18 semester hours (the range is from 12 to 27), 15 per cent of the total four-year program, leaving 100 hours or more for study in the academic fields.

Number, Types, and Accreditation
of Teacher Education Institutions

The number of approved teacher education institutions has declined substantially in recent years. The total number of colleges and universities approved for teacher education dropped from 1,218 in 1957 to 1,147 in 1959, a decrease of 71. The number of approved institutions ranges from one in each of four states (Alaska, Hawaii, Nevada, and Wyoming) to 82 in Pennsylvania. The median number in a state is 22.

Among the 1,147 institutions in 1959, there were 90 public teachers colleges, a decrease of 23, and nine private teachers colleges, a decrease of four, for a grand total of 99, a decrease of 27 since 1957. (A teachers college is defined as a separate, single-purpose institution, as provided in legislation establishing its function, with teachers college in its name; a state college of education; or a four-year normal school operating as a separate institution.)

A quick check of the numbers of teachers colleges in 1960 indicates that the number of state teachers colleges has dropped to 73. (The 14 Pennsylvania state teachers colleges have become state colleges; the 12 New York state teachers colleges have become colleges of education but, of course, remain in this category.) Apparently, there are in 1960 twelve private teachers colleges, making a total of 85 public and private teachers colleges.

The 1960 list of approved teacher education institutions also includes 221 universities (93 public and 128 private), 705 general or liberal arts colleges (154 public and 551 private), 38 technical schools, 73 junior colleges, and 11 unclassified schools.

There has been a steady changeover from state teachers colleges to state (general) colleges during the past decade. Since 1951 a total of 73 teachers colleges and normal schools have become state colleges or universities, and two others have disappeared through mergers. The states in which this change has occurred and the number of institutions affected are Alabama, 5; Connecticut, 4; District of Columbia, 2 (through the merging of two teachers colleges as a result of school integration); Illinois, 1; Kansas, 1; Michigan, 4; Minnesota, 5; Mississippi, 1; Missouri, 2 (through the merging of two St. Louis teachers colleges as a result of integration); New Jersey, 6; North Carolina, 2; Texas, 3; Wisconsin, 27 (19 normal schools became junior colleges and eight state teachers colleges became state colleges); and Pennsylvania, 14. In several states (notably Illinois, Michigan, and Ohio), the original normal schools over the years have evolved into state teachers colleges, into state colleges, and then into state universities.

This is a continuation of a trend away from the single-purpose teacher education institution which began in earnest about 1930. Hughes[4] reports that 33 state teachers colleges were changed to state colleges between 1931 and 1950. Since 1930, therefore, at least 106 teachers colleges and normal schools became state colleges, with several later becoming state universities. The evolution of normal schools into degree-granting state teachers colleges was even more abrupt, especially during the years from 1910 to 1950, when 134 such conversions were made, 103 of these occurring in the two decades from 1920 to 1940.[5] Many interpretations have been given to these shifts, especially the shift from teachers colleges to state colleges. The real explanation appears to hinge upon two factors: (1) the trend toward the professionalizaton of teaching, which has resulted in the adoption in most states of college degrees and the completion of prescribed curricula (a practice which obtains in all recognized professions) for beginning teachers, and thus in the growing acceptance of teacher education as an integral part of higher education and as an accepted professional discipline; and (2) in recent years, the pressures of increased enrollments which have forced state legislatures to consider two alternatives: (a) to authorize the building of new campuses, or (b) to utilize existing ones by converting single-purpose

[4] Rees H. Hughes, "Changing Status of Teacher Education Institutions," *Journal of Teacher Education* 2: 48-50; March 1951.
[5] *Ibid.*

teachers colleges into general or multiple-purpose colleges. The choice of the latter alternative as being more economical and feasible obviously helps to explain the widespread conversions described above.

It is doubtless true that the change of name from state teachers college to state college does not necessarily mean an immediate change in function. Thus, many of the newly created state colleges may, in fact, remain for several years as institutions devoted primarily to teacher education. The same kind of difficulty in classifying institutions is encountered with some institutions designated as "universities." Some of these, when their programs and functions are examined, are actually general or liberal arts colleges.

Another trend of significance is the decrease in the number (108) of junior colleges approved for teacher education between 1957 and 1959. This may be attributed to the establishment of the degree as the minimum for teacher certification in all but ten states. This trend to drop junior colleges from lists of approved institutions, in terms of their offering full programs for regular certification, will doubtless continue.

The types of accreditation of these 1,147 institutions in 1959 were as follows: accreditation by the state education agency, 1,147; by regional associations, 956; by the National Council for Accreditation of Teacher Education, 317. Thus, there were only 191 institutions engaging in teacher education which did not achieve accreditation by their regional associations, but since certification requirements are always stated as minima, a better measure is what colleges and universities actually require.

Curricular Requirements

An analysis of 294 institutions accredited by the NCATE in 1957-58 provides the most extensive data available and a reasonably accurate profile of teacher education in the United States. Although this is a minority of the institutions engaged in educating teachers, these 294 institutions prepare some two-thirds of the new teachers graduated each year.

The median requirements of these 294 institutions in professional education (see Table 19-2) for elementary-school teachers was 34 semester hours (of which 8 are in student teaching), with a range of from 18 to 69 hours; 7 of every 10 of these 294 institutions ranged in requirements from 20 to 40 hours, and three required 60 hours or more. For high-school teachers, the median requirement was 23 semester hours (of which **7** were in student teaching), with the range from 10 to 51 hours.

The extreme cases, such as the three institutions requiring 60 or more hours in education for elementary-school teachers and the one requiring 51 hours for high-school teachers, tend to be singled out and held up as proof of too much methodology in teacher education. Such extremes are indefensible. The true picture, however, is to be drawn from the fact that the typical practice is 34 hours for elementary-school teachers and 23 hours for high-school teachers, a little more than a fourth and a little less than one-fifth, respectively, of the degree programs.

TABLE 19-2

COMPOSITE OF CENTRAL TENDENCIES AND RANGES OF SEMESTER-HOUR REQUIREMENTS IN THE TEACHER EDUCATION PROGRAMS OF NCATE-ACCREDITED INSTITUTIONS

	Programs for Elementary Teachers				Total No. of Institutions Reporting	Programs for Secondary Teaching Majors		Total No. of Institutions Reporting
	Mean	Median	Mode	Range		Median	Range	
Professional Education	34.8	34	36	18-69	287	23	10-51	275
General Education*	—	46	—	11-97	292	46	11-97	292
Teaching Major								
Agriculture						43	24-99	58
Art						36	12-93	207
Business						36	18-75	215
English						30	18-64	249
Foreign								
Languages ...						25	18-68	210
History						30	18-64	155
Home Economics						40	24-78	189
Industrial Arts ..						37	18-79	149
Mathematics ...						27	18-64	251
Music						40	24-99	227
Physical Education						34	18-99	221
Science						31	18-81	257
Social Science ...						35	18-62	152

* Report is for elementary and secondary teachers.

In general education (see Table 19-2) the 294 institutions typically required about 46 semester hours for both elementary-school and secondary-school teachers. For teaching-field majors for high-school teachers, the median requirements ranged from 25 semester hours in foreign languages to 43 in agriculture.[6]

[6] "Analysis of Quantitative Requirements in Teacher Education Programs of 294 Colleges and Universities," *The Education of Teachers: Curriculum Programs*, Report of the Kansas Conference (Washington, D. C.: National Commission on Teacher Education and Professional Standards, National Education Association, 1959), pp. 173-186.

CHAPTER TWENTY

Who Certifies Our Teachers— and How?

A great area of controversy in the education of teachers is the licensure process. The critics have repeatedly charged that the professors of education have secured a strangle hold on education in our lower schools by exercising control over the teacher certification requirements set by the respective state boards or departments of education; and that, as pointed out in the preceding chapter, their chief interest has been to prescribe excessive requirements in education courses. This controversy, inevitably, was discussed in the three cooperative conferences. Perhaps a look at the licensure process will help in understanding the continual feuding about it.

Minimum Requirements of States

By September 1, 1961, a total of 43 states and territories (hereafter "state" will be used to designate the 50 states, the District of Columbia, and Puerto Rico) will be enforcing the minimum requirement of the bachelor's degree for the lowest regular certificate for beginning elementary-school teachers; and all states will be enforcing this minimum for high-school teachers.[1] Arkansas and Iowa began enforcing the degree requirement in September 1960; Missouri adopted the degree minimum, effective in 1961. Thus, there remain nine states yet to establish the degree minimum for beginning elementary-school teachers. These states, with their semester-hour requirements, are as

[1] This survey has drawn heavily upon Chapter 1 of W. Earl Armstrong and T. M. Stinnett, *A Manual on Certification Requirements for School Personnel in the United States,* 1959 Edition (Washington, D. C.: National Commission on Teacher Education and Professional Standards, National Education Association, 1959), pp. 1-54. New material, based upon information supplied by the respective state directors of teacher education and certification on changes since the publication of the 1959 *Manual,* has been included. Thus, the survey reflects existing conditions as of March 1960.

follows: Alaska, 90; Colorado, 60; Maine, 96; Montana, 64; Nebraska, 40; North Dakota, 32; Puerto Rico, 67; South Dakota, 60; and Wisconsin, 64.[2] Three states (Arizona, District of Columbia, and California) require the minimum of five years of college preparation for beginning high-school teachers. Also, five states (Connecticut, Indiana, New York, Oregon, and Washington) which enforce the bachelor's degree as a minimum for beginning teachers mandate completion of the fifth year of college work within a specified period after initial service.

TABLE 20-1

MINIMUM REQUIREMENTS FOR LOWEST REGULAR TEACHING CERTIFICATES FOR PREPARING TEACHERS AS OF SEPTEMBER 1, 1961

	Elementary School			High School		
State	Degree or Number of Semester Hours Required	Professional Education Required, Semester Hours (Total)	Directed Teaching Required, Semester Hours (Included in Col. 6)	Degree or Number of College Years Required	Professional Education Required, Semester Hours (Total)	Directed Teaching Required, Semester Hours (Included in Col. 6)
1	2	3	4	5	6	7
Alabama	B	30	3	B	24	3
Alaska	90	16	4	B	16	4
Arizona	B	18	6	5	18	6
Arkansas	B	12	3	B	12	3
California	B	24	8	5	22	6
Colorado	60	20	4	B	20	4
Connecticut	B	30	6	B	18	6
Delaware	B	30	6	B	18	6
District of Columbia	B	24	6	5	18	6
Florida	B	20	6	B	20	6
Georgia	B	18	6	B	18	6
Hawaii	B	18	AC	B	18	AC
Idaho	B	20	6	B	20	6
Illinois	B	16	5	B	16	5
Indiana	B	30	6	B	18	5
Iowa	B	20	5	B	20	5
Kansas	B	24	5	B	20	5
Kentucky	B	24	8	B	17	8
Louisiana	B	24	4	B	18	4

[2] No effort is made here to delineate deviations from the established degree minimums, which exist in some states, or to identify those states which still issue emergency certificates. For a discussion of these factors, see p. 3 of the *Manual*.

TABLE 20-1 *(cont.)*

	Elementary School			High School		
State	Degree or Number of Semester Hours Required	Profes- sional Education Required, Semester Hours (Total)	Directed Teaching Required, Semester Hours (Included in Col. 6)	Degree or Number of College Years Required	Profes- sional Education Required, Semester Hours (Total)	Directed Teaching Required, Semester Hours (Included in Col. 6)
1	2	3	4	5	6	7
Maine	96	AC	AC	B	12	0
Maryland	B	32	6	B	16	3
Massachusetts	B	18	2	B	12	2
Michigan	B	20	5	B	20	5
Minnesota	B	30	6	B	18	4
Mississippi	B	36	6	B	18	6
Missouri	B	18	5	B	18	5
Montana	64	AC	AC	B	AC	AC
Nebraska	40	8	3	B	18	3
Nevada	B	30	4	B	18	4
New Hampshire	B	AC	6	B	21	6
New Jersey	B	30	6	B	18	6
New Mexico	B	24	6	B	18	6
New York	B	36	12	B	18	6
North Carolina	B	18	3	B	18	3
North Dakota	32	16	3	B	16	3
Ohio	B	28	6	B	17	6
Oklahoma	B	21	6	B	21	6
Oregon	B	20	4	B	24	6
Pennsylvania	B	18	6	B	18	6
Puerto Rico	67	30	6	B	21	5
Rhode Island	B	30	6	B	18	6
South Carolina	B	21	6	B	18	6
South Dakota	60	15	3	B	20	5
Tennessee	B	24	4	B	24	4
Texas	B	24	6	B	24	6
Utah	B	30	8	B	22	9
Vermont	B	18	6	B	18	6
Virginia	B	18	6	B	15	4-6
Washington	B	27	10	B	27	10
West Virginia	B	20	5	B	20	5
Wisconsin	64	26	8	B	18	5
Wyoming	B	20	C	B	20	C

LEGEND: AC means approved curriculum; B means bachelor's degree of specified preparation; 5 means degree plus a fifth year of approved preparation, not necessarily completion of the master's degree; C means a course.

SOURCE: This table is adapted from *A Manual on Certification Requirements for School Personnel in the United States,* 1959 Edition, Table III, p. 19.

Authority for Certification

Authority for fixing requirements for issuing, reissuing, and revoking teachers' certificates is almost completely vested by legislative authority in the respective state departments or state boards of education. Only five states (Colorado, Indiana, Montana, Nebraska, and North Dakota) report that their legislatures retain some measure of the certification authority in law. In the laws vesting authority in the state education agencies, certain general specifications are retained in the law in most states. These specifications usually deal with age, citizenship, health, oaths, and special course requirements (notably state history and constitution).

In nine states, the certification authority is shared to some degree with other agencies. In seven states, certain cities are authorized to issue certificates to their teachers: Colorado (first-class districts), Delaware (Wilmington), Illinois (Chicago), Maryland (Baltimore), New York (New York City and Buffalo), North Dakota (Fargo), and Oregon (Portland).

In four states, certain state colleges and universities are authorized to issue certificates to their teacher education graduates: Colorado (state teachers colleges), Kansas (must grant one certificate to Bachelor of Science in Education graduates of three state colleges), Missouri (the University of Missouri, Lincoln University, and five state colleges are authorized to issue certificates to their graduates), and North Dakota (diplomas of graduates of state colleges are accepted as certificates).

The following excerpts from two state laws are indicative of the broad nature of legislative grants of authority:

Alabama. The State Board of Education . . . shall prescribe rules and regulations governing the training and certification of teachers in public schools of the state. . . . The State Board of Education . . . shall have full power and authority to promulgate and adopt rules and regulations governing the issuance of certificates.

Kansas. The State Superintendent of Public Instruction, subject to the approval of the State Board of Education, is authorized to make rules and regulations covering the issuance, renewal, revival, and registration of certificates for teachers, supervisors, and administrative officers of elementary and secondary public schools in the state of Kansas, including kindergarten, common or elementary schools, junior high schools, high schools, and public junior colleges.

School Personnel Required to Hold Certificates

There are legal provisions in all states requiring certain public-school personnel to hold certificates issued by the designated state education agency. There is some variation among the states regarding what public-school personnel are required to hold certificates. All states require teachers, administrators, and special school-service personnel in the public elementary and secondary schools to hold certificates; 15 states require public nursery-school teachers and 40 states require public kindergarten teachers to do so. Probably all states maintaining nursery and kindergarten schools at public expense require certification of teachers in such schools. Fourteen states require teachers in publicly supported junior colleges to hold certificates. In general, these are states in which the junior colleges are a part of the public-school system, usually being maintained by the local school districts as an extension of secondary education, although there are exceptions to this. Four states require teachers in the state teachers colleges to hold certificates.

Only 13 states, either by law or regulation, require teachers in both private and parochial schools—at some school level—to hold certificates.

The predominant practice among states regarding certification of teachers in privately supported and controlled schools is either to require certification only in cases where the school seeks accreditation by the state or to issue certificates upon the voluntary requests of teachers in private schools.

TABLE 20-2

MINIMUM NUMBER OF COLLEGE YEARS OF PREPARATION REQUIRED
BY STATES AND TERRITORIES FOR INITIAL CERTIFICATES IN 1961

College Years of Preparation	Elementary-School Teachers	High-School Teachers	Elementary-School Principals	High-School Principals	Superintendents of Schools
	Number of States and Territories Requiring				
Six	0	0	0	0	3
Five Plus	0	0	3	5	4
Five	0	3	23	30	35
Four Plus	0	0	13	11	5
Four	43	49	8	5	3
Three Plus	2	0	3	0	0
Two Plus	5	0	0	0	0
One Plus	2	0	0	0	0
No Certificate for Position Issued	0	0	2	1	2
TOTALS	52	52	52	52	52

Who Participates in Setting Requirements?

In one form or another, the teaching profession has broad recommendatory powers in almost all states regarding teacher education requirements. As early as 1930, the pressures surrounding the formulation and enforcement of teacher education and certification requirements had grown to such proportions that the state education agencies began to seek means of democratizing the procedures. Logically, they turned to representatives of the profession from professional organizations and colleges and universities. Advisory councils on teacher education and certification have been in existence in most states for many years, as a means of providing participation of the profession in formulating certification requirements.

In 1960, all but six states reported some form of advisory group. Thirty-six states reported advisory councils or committees by these names. Four states (Colorado, Hawaii, New Jersey, and Texas) reported state boards of examiners. The Indiana Teacher Training and Licensing Commission is a legal committee of the State Board of Education; Illinois has a state teacher certification board and also an advisory council; and Hawaii has a coordinating committee. The state TEPS commission serves the council function in five states (Maryland, Oklahoma, Vermont, Wisconsin, and Wyoming), and one state (Delaware) reported the organization of a council in process.

In nine states (Colorado, Florida, Hawaii, Illinois, Indiana, Kentucky, New Hampshire, Tennessee, and Texas) the councils or boards of examiners are created by law. The others are extralegal or voluntary organizations.

In size the councils range from eight to 225 members; the median number of members is 21. A typical pattern of membership is for each teacher education institution to have one representative, for the state education association and its affiliated special-field associations or departments to have several representatives, and for the state director of teacher education and certification to serve as chairman (10 states), secretary (20 states), or member ex-officio (8 states). Typically, also, members are appointed by the state board of education or by the state superintendent of public instruction or commissioner of education (21 states).

The complaints of the critics tend to focus on the absence of subject-matter professors from these advisory bodies. This is a valid criticism, although the alleged reasons for their nonparticipation are often not. As has been pointed out, typically, representation is provided for each approved teacher education college or university in a given state. Generally, the college presidents have appointed their deans of education as their institutions' representatives on the advisory council. This seems quite logical, and it would work if each president would follow up by establishing machinery on the campus which would be representative of the faculty as a whole in matters having to do with teacher education. In this manner, an institution's representative on the state's advisory council could speak for the total institution. This is now being done in a large number of institutions. A recent survey by the Council on Cooperation in Teacher Education revealed that nearly 400 colleges and universities have already set up such cooperative machinery.

The absence of representatives of the liberal arts on these councils has been criticized, and justly so. State boards of education are now moving to correct this situation by specifying that such representatives be included in the membership of the councils.

Types of Certificates Issued by the States

The types of certificates issued to school personnel by the states may be classified under three categories: (1) according to the term of duration of validity; (2) according to levels of preparation; and (3) according to authorization of teaching position or assignment.

Life and Permanent Certificates. A total of 27 states issue life or permanent certificates. The permanent certificate usually is not a life certificate, remaining valid only so long as the holder teaches continuously or is not out of teaching beyond a specified number of years or completes additional college work.

Blanket Certificates. Sixteen states issue blanket or general high-school certificates on which teaching fields and subjects, which the holder is qualified to teach according to the requirements of the given state, are not endorsed. This does not mean that a holder is authorized to teach any and all fields, as it is often interpreted. All states have teaching-field prescriptions which teachers must meet to be legally assigned to teach a particular subject. In some states these prescriptions are set forth in the certification regulations; sometimes they are given in the accrediting requirements of the state. The enforcement of the teaching assignment in the case of the blanket certificate is usually left to the employing school officers and to the accrediting authorities, sometimes aided by regulations for allotment of state financial aid.

Endorsed Certificates. The predominant practice among the states is the issuance of endorsed certificates, which means that one or more teaching fields or subjects for which the holder meets the specified preparation requirements of the state are endorsed on the certificate as evidence to the employing school official of the qualifications of the teacher for assignment. Thirty-seven states issue this type of certificate on which the academic teaching fields are endorsed; 31 states endorse special fields as well on the high-school certificate, while 13 states issue a separate certificate for each special field.

Certificates Based on Examinations. Sixteen states report that some use of examinations, bearing on certification, is made (Colorado, District of Columbia, Florida, Illinois, Kansas, Maine, Missouri, New Hampshire, New Jersey, Nevada, New York, Oklahoma, South Carolina, Utah, West Virginia, and Wyoming). In addition, West Virginia and Wisconsin have developed a plan for use of proficiency examinations for holders of the bachelor's degree. Also, Kansas reported authority to provide examinations to permit a licensed teacher to qualify for additional teaching fields, but this procedure is rarely used. Actually, only Missouri uses the examination for initial certification purposes without substantial prerequisites. In Missouri, county superintendents are authorized to conduct examination for elementary-school teachers in rural schools, with high-school graduation as the prerequisite. Florida uses the National Teacher Examinations to validate credentials of out-of-state applicants from unaccredited institutions. Illinois will certify elementary-school teachers who have completed two years of college work on the basis of a qualifying examination.

Maine has made provision for use of examinations to certify superintendents who have completed a bachelor's degree, 18 semester hours in education, and three years of teaching experience. New York reported some use of examinations to certify foreign language teachers. These examinations are in addition to the requirements which other high-school teachers must meet. Utah has a legislative provision which permits holders of regular elementary-school certificates to qualify for teaching in kindergarten by examination. West Virginia adopted in 1958 a provision permitting liberal arts graduates to qualify for provisional certificates by use of the National Teacher Examinations, and for inservice teachers to qualify for additional fields of authorization.

South Carolina uses the National Teacher Examinations as a qualifying examination for certification of graduates of approved teacher education programs. Also, holders of regular certificates may earn higher-grade certificates by achieving specified scores on the National Teacher Examinations. Oklahoma, Nevada, New Jersey, and Wyoming permit examinations in lieu of a credit course to satisfy requirements for special courses such as state history, constitution, and health education. New Hampshire occasionally employs proficiency examinations to satisfy some professional education requirements.

Of the states making some use of examinations in certification, in all except two, Illinois and Missouri, the examinations must be classified as proficiency examinations in either of these two categories: (1) those by which applicants who meet degree or minimum collegiate years of preparation for regular certificates, but who do not meet specified professional education or teaching-field requirements in certain academic or general fields; and (2) those by which applicants may demonstrate competence to have certain prescribed courses waived (New Jersey, Nevada, Oklahoma, and Wyoming). Several state departments of education are known to be exploring the idea of either proficiency or qualifying examinations.

CHAPTER TWENTY-ONE

Outcomes of Group Discussions—
Analysis in Brief

Bowling Green

Most participants agreed that teacher education programs should insist that prospective teachers be well educated as well as technically trained.

The consensus was reached that professional educators and other scholars from the areas of science, humanities, and social sciences should cooperate in developing better teacher education programs through some form of all-college or all-university planning.

The development of the American school system and its purposes were held to be of central importance and, therefore, should also be central in any and all considerations respective to the education of teachers.

An apparent theme running through much of the discussion was that the development of understanding was more important than the reaching of agreements.

The great diversity of American educational institutions, although considered somewhat of a barrier, was felt by many to be a great asset and one which could well become a basis of strength through the development of appropriate interrelationships.

There was a strong sense of acceptance of responsibility among the participants, especially for developing cooperation. Teacher education was deemed too important to be the sole responsibility of one select group, even though fixed responsibility for leadership and the administrative aspects of teacher education programs should reside in colleges of education or their equivalents.

Appropriate relationships between and among teacher education, accreditation, and certification were held to be imperatives; and broad representation, including liberal arts, was urged in establishing accreditation and certification procedures.

There was complete agreement that the cooperative endeavor between and among the various learned societies and professional educators should proceed.

Kansas

The Kansas Conference was almost completely unanimous in recommending cooperative approaches to planning the teacher education curriculum. Four of the groups suggested specific organizational approaches. Only two of the groups expressed a reservation that the college of education might lose sight of its ultimate responsibility for the program.

A number of the groups spoke of the importance of selective admission and guidance procedures in the teacher education program. A feeling was commonly expressed that quality had to be raised. Early identification of prospective teachers was felt desirable.

A large number of the groups stressed the importance of foreign languages as a part of the general education of teachers. Some would require it; others thought such a requirement ought to be a goal; a minority felt that foreign language competence should not be required at all.

The need for a fifth year of collegiate preparation of teachers was often mentioned. There was wide agreement that four years allowed insufficient time to provide adequate general education and the professional sequence. Most groups stressed the importance of providing academic courses in the fifth year. The importance of having teaching experience before the fifth year was often mentioned. Some felt that special academic courses for teachers might be desirable.

There was general agreement that a substantial portion of the four-year program should be devoted to general education—the humanities, the social sciences, and the natural sciences, including mathematics. Some proposed a series of broad, integrated courses. Others objected, urging that general education should provide a basis for specialization and that single disciplinary courses were best. Special mention was made of the importance of improving English in the general education sequence; foreign languages and the study of foreign cultures were also mentioned. In general, the groups felt that institutions should work out their own programs and that flexibility in program development was very important.

Nearly all groups thought that teachers should have a substantial degree of academic specialization in addition to general and specialized education. The notion seemed to be that all teachers should have a respectable major. This applied to elementary-school teachers as well as to secondary-school teachers. Others suggested that something like the equivalent of a major would be feasible, but studies in broader areas and in interdisciplinary areas should be permitted. A minority felt that specialization for elementary-school teachers, except in such fields as child psychology and human growth and development, was not practical or necessary.

In professional education, most groups proposed that the historical, sociological, psychological, and philosophical foundations of education be included. In addition, appropriate courses in methods and student teaching were recommended. Most groups agreed that elementary-school teachers need more methods courses, but some disagreed. One group thought that improvement could be achieved by combining a study of teaching methods and student teaching. There was divergence of opinion on when to begin professional courses; most groups agreed on the junior year, but several urged early admission to teaching majors and, particularly, early teaching experiences.

Ten groups mentioned the improvement of college instruction.

San Diego

There was general concern that certification not be considered separately, but in a context which includes teacher education, accreditation, and other related areas of professional concern.

Most felt that authority for initial certification should be vested with a legal agency, but that such an agency should avail itself of counsel from advisory groups chosen from the profession at large.

There was considerable support given to the idea that initial certification should be based upon recommendation of accredited institutions possessing programs planned on an institution-wide basis.

Support was given to the idea that the state (legal agency) should not go beyond the issuing of the first license, and that beyond the first license the profession should set standards for specialization and enforce them. Some felt, however, that the profession was not ready for such a step; others were concerned about too much control being vested with too small a group.

There was a tendency to agree that there should be fixed responsibility for teacher education programs in a professional college or its equivalent, but that there should be great flexibility. Apparently there was a tendency to agree that teacher education programs should be based more upon the needs of individual students—that is, upon proficiencies rather than upon college credits or degrees, or both. Many felt that maturity had not always been given desirable consideration.

Some groups advocated the establishment of state commissions to assure appropriate relationships between and among the various agencies concerned with teacher education and certification.

Concern was expressed that certain basic organizational structures related to education, including reorganization of school districts, should be fully realized before special types of certificates could be dropped.

The problem of misassignment of teachers obviously disturbed a great many of the participants. Most felt that this problem would have to be approached through a combination of steps rather than by depending entirely upon one avenue of control.

At least one group was deeply concerned that no person receive a professional certificate until he is also on tenure, and vice versa.

The National Council for Accreditation of Teacher Education was given considerable time and vocal encouragement at this conference. Many felt that this instrumentality could, with appropriate support, soon provide the recognized basis for reciprocity in teacher certification among all the states. There was a strong feeling on the part of some individuals that the council should have more representation from the liberal arts.

A few groups advocated greater experimentation, especially with proficiency tests and internships; however, a majority of the groups at least implied that any such experimentation should be done within the confines of a fixed responsibility for teacher education.

Many other items were mentioned, such as the relationship of certification to ethics. Substandard certification was deplored, and especially the way it has been handled in some cases; there was a call for the improvement of teacher education; and several groups felt that greater attention should be given to the development of a comprehensive five-year teacher education program.

The most common area of agreement in the San Diego Conference, as in the Bowling Green and Kansas Conferences, was again the importance of maintaining the cooperative attitude among the various segments of the profession interested in teacher education. Considerable concern was expressed that, although cooperation seemed apparent at the national level, there was much need to develop procedures and projects whereby this cooperative process would become much more diffused, especially at the local, state, and institutional levels.

Appendix I

DISTRIBUTION OF PARTICIPANTS IN THE COOPERATIVE CONFERENCES

(Bowling Green, Kansas, 1960 Regionals, and San Diego)

Position	Bowling Green	Kansas	1960 Regional Conferences	San Diego	Totals
Liberal Arts	162	215	145	197	719
Education	264	271	502	199	1,236
Elementary- and Secondary-School Teachers	297	284	296	276	1,153
School Administrators	102	118	193	127	540
State Departments of Education	49	52	75	56	232
State Education Associations	60	55	101	84	300
Lay People	16	19	20	22	77
Student NEA Members	75	86	44	80	285
GRAND TOTAL					4,542

Appendix II

The New York Times, Sunday, July 6, 1958

EDUCATION IN REVIEW [1]

Scholars and Teachers Find a Common Ground in a Debate on Training

by Loren B. Pope

The leaders of a divided educational world went to Bowling Green expecting a battle of the decades on the issue of subject matter versus professional training in the preparation of public school teachers. Instead, both sides were pleased to discover they were fighting on the same side. Both want the school teacher to be well educated as well as technically trained.

The discovery produced such a strong, new sense of co-operation that both professional educators and scholars in the sciences and humanities have pronounced the week's reconciliation and collaboration a more important event than the 1955 White House Conference on Education.

This meeting was the first time in half a century of feuding and epithets that the school teachers and teacher education officials had met on a grand scale with the liberal arts people for a common discussion of teacher education needs.

It grew out of a desire of a few persons on both sides of a divided educational world to talk things out. . . . The professional societies in the sciences and the humanities agreed to be cosponsors, and a hundred of the nation's leading universities sent representatives.

.   .   .

The liberal arts professors, arriving at Bowling Green, edgily expected a fight on the issue described in the old story that the professional educator argues that a teacher doesn't teach math; she teaches Mary. The liberal arts man replies: Why not teach Mary math?

.   .   .

Instead, the liberal arts people found the teacher education officials do want to teach Mary math. Neither side, however, expects agreement now on specific teacher education programs to do this. For one thing, they don't anticipate resolving overnight a debate of decades. For another, the great diversity of American educational institutions is a barrier.

The one really important thing to them is the fact that both sides have found they want to, and can, work together. This apparent willingness and ability of the two long-divided parts of the education world to collaborate, the conference participants said, is a development of central importance to the American school system.

[1] Reproduced by permission of the *New York Times*.

174

The mood for co-operation was set at the conference's start. Dr. T. M. Stinnett, executive secretary of the sponsoring NEA Commission on Teacher Education, made it clear the teachers were interested in the scholars' ideas.

.   .   .

Each side made some mutually reassuring commitments on matters of principle. The teacher education group, for its part, declared in favor of a well-rounded education, plus depth of learning in their specialties for all school teachers, and higher standards for the colleges that train them. . . .

Many of the state teacher groups also voted at Bowling Green to ask the liberal arts professors to help plan both the teacher education curricula and state certification requirements. This is something the liberal arts camp has long declared must be done if teacher education is to be improved.

In return, the science professors gave their tacit blessing to curricula for high school science teachers that "recognize" and favor good professional education courses.

The liberal arts professors, to meet the teachers halfway, must now convert their colleagues at home to co-operation with "those teacher education people." The Bowling Green meeting, with the prestige lent by participation of the learned societies and the name universities, is expected to help make that collaboration a professionally respectable activity for the scholars, and therefore easier.

Over all, both sides at the Bowling Green Conference confessed a sense of guilt for the neglect that has divided and hurt the education world. Both demonstrated a lively conviction that the education of teachers is too important to the nation to be left to the sole jurisdiction of either the liberal arts or the teacher education group by itself. There was a sense of need for the strength of union—to achieve the teacher education goals which the liberal arts group has not been able to force by itself, and to win the public support for education which the organized school teachers have not been able to do even in these times.

Appendix III

LIST OF COSPONSORING AND COOPERATING ORGANIZATIONS

(Bowling Green, Kansas, and San Diego Conferences)

Cosponsoring Organizations

American Association for the Advancement of Science
American Association of Colleges for Teacher Education
American Council of Learned Societies
Association of American Colleges, Commission on Teacher Education
Council on Cooperation in Teacher Education, American Council on Education
National Academy of Sciences-National Research Council
National Association of State Directors of Teacher Education and Certification
National Commission on Teacher Education and Professional Standards
National Council for Accreditation of Teacher Education

Cooperating Organizations

American Association for Health, Physical Education, and Recreation (NEA)
American Association for Jewish Education
American Association of Collegiate Registrars and Admissions Officers
American Association of Land-Grant Colleges and State Universities and the State Universities Association, Committee on Teacher Education
American Association of Physics Teachers
American Association of School Administrators (NEA)
American Association of School Personnel Administrators
American Chemical Society
American Economic Association
American Foundation for the Blind, Inc.
American Geographical Society
American Geological Institute
American Geophysical Union
American Historical Association
American Home Economics Association
American Industrial Arts Association
American Institute of Biological Sciences
American Institute of Physics
American Library Association
American Medical Association
American Personnel and Guidance Association
American Philological Association
American Philosophical Association
American Psychological Association
American Society for Engineering Education

American Sociological Association
Association for Asian Studies, Inc.
Association for Childhood Education International
Association for Higher Education (NEA)
Association for Student Teaching
Association for Supervision and Curriculum Development (NEA)
Association of Graduate Schools in the Association of American Universities
College Art Association of America
College English Association, Inc.
Conference Board of the Mathematical Sciences, American Mathematical Society
Council for Basic Education
Council for Exceptional Children (NEA)
Department of Audio-Visual Instruction (NEA)
Department of Classroom Teachers (NEA)
Department of Elementary School Principals (NEA)
Department of Home Economics (NEA)
Department of Rural Education (NEA)
Federation of American Societies for Experimental Biology
Modern Language Association of America
Music Educators National Conference (NEA)
National Art Education Association (NEA)
National Association for Research in Science Teaching
National Association of Biology Teachers
National Association of Journalism Directors (NEA)
National Association of Public School Adult Educators (NEA)
National Association of Schools of Music
National Association of Secondary-School Principals (NEA)
National Association of Women Deans and Counselors (NEA)
National Aviation Education Council
National Catholic Educational Association
National Commission for the Defense of Democracy Through Education
National Commission on Safety Education (NEA)
National Council for the Social Studies (NEA)
National Council of Independent Schools, Inc.
National Council of Teachers of English
National Council of Teachers of Mathematics (NEA)
National Institutional Teacher Placement Association
National League of Teachers Associations
National Science Teachers Association (NEA)
National Society of College Teachers of Education
National Society of Professional Engineers
Scientific Manpower Commission
Seventh-Day Adventists General Conference, Department of Education
Sister-Formation Conference, National Catholic Educational Association
Society of American Bacteriologists
Speech Association of America
United Business Education Association (NEA)

SPECTRUM PAPERBACKS

Other SPECTRUM Books . . . quality paperbacks that meet the highest standards of scholarship and integrity.